Praise for *A Commuter's Guide to Enlightenment*

"This is a beautifully explicated work founded in Sufi tradition. Whether you are looking for some peace of mind to get you through your daily commute, or if you are pursuing a much deeper understanding of life, this book will serve you outstandingly. Keep this book around for a long time. You never know when some portion of it will begin to make new sense to you."

—Jerry Katz, editor, *One: Essential Writings on Nonduality*

"In this unique travel guide, Dr. Bitkoff teaches the basics of spiritual growth using allegory, metaphor, narrative, and common sense. While life passes all around us, we are taught that our attitudes and beliefs help determine what we see, hear, and feel. Dr. Bitkoff helps us to become aware of the relationship between our external environment and internal response. He helps us approach the twists and turns in life by providing intellectual, emotional, and spiritual choices that we either never learned or simply failed to pay attention to. Let Dr. Bitkoff be your driving instructor."

—Michael Greenstein, MS, CEO,
a hospital administrator in the New York state/New Jersey
mental health systems

D1563710

A

COMMUTER'S

GUIDE

to

enlightenment

About the Author

Stewart Bitkoff, a doctoral graduate in education, grew up in New York City and spent most of his professional career living and working in the New York City area. An expert in therapeutic recreation and psychiatric rehabilitation and treatment, Dr. Bitkoff has been on the faculty or served as a field instructor for New York University, Herbert H. Lehman College, Iona College, the College of New Rochelle, East Stroudsburg University, and Northampton Community College.

He has written many works centering on the topic of the completed person and the original human development system. For years, Dr. Bitkoff studied in two modern mystical schools. Professionally, he has worked to help the mentally ill integrate their altered state of consciousness into the physical world; he is presently guiding children and their families as a behavioral consultant. Dr. Bitkoff also serves on the board of directors of the Shooting for the Moon Spiritual Development Center in Snydersville, Pennsylvania.

Please visit his website at www.thedeeganproject.com.

A

COMMUTER'S

GUIDE

 to

enlightenment

DR. STEWART BITKOFF

Llewellyn Publications
Woodbury, Minnesota

First Edition
First Printing, 2008
Cover art © 2007 BrandX Pictures
Cover design by Ellen Dahl
Editing by Brett Fechheimer
Llewellyn is a registered trademark of Llewellyn Worldwide, Ltd.

Bitkoff, Stewart, 1946–
   A commuter's guide to enlightenment / Stewart Bitkoff. — 1st ed.
      p.   cm.
   Includes bibliographical references.
   ISBN 978-0-7387-1263-5
   1. Sufism—Doctrines. I. Title.
   BP189.3.B55 2008
   297.4'4—dc22
                              2007050296

Llewellyn Worldwide does not participate in, endorse, or have any authority or responsibility concerning private business transactions between our authors and the public.

   All mail addressed to the author is forwarded but the publisher cannot, unless specifically instructed by the author, give out an address or phone number.

   Any Internet references contained in this work are current at publication time, but the publisher cannot guarantee that a specific location will continue to be maintained. Please refer to the publisher's website for links to authors' websites and other sources.

Llewellyn Publications
A Division of Llewellyn Worldwide, Ltd.
2143 Wooddale Drive, Dept. 978-0-7387-1263-5
Woodbury, Minnesota 55125-2989, U.S.A.
www.llewellyn.com
Printed in the United States of America

To Write to the Author

If you wish to contact the author or would like more information about this book, please write to the author in care of Llewellyn Worldwide and we will forward your request. Both the author and publisher appreciate hearing from you and learning of your enjoyment of this book and how it has helped you. Llewellyn Worldwide cannot guarantee that every letter written to the author can be answered, but all will be forwarded. Please write to:

Stewart Bitkoff
℅ Llewellyn Worldwide
2143 Wooddale Drive. 978-0-7387-1263-5
Woodbury, MN 55125-2989, U.S.A.

Please enclose a self-addressed stamped envelope for reply, or $1.00 to cover costs. If outside the USA, enclose international postal reply coupon.

For Llewellyn's free full-color catalog, write to *New Worlds* at the above address, or call 1-877-NEW-WRLD.

This work is dedicated to Amjed
and the other hidden friends of humanity,
without whom this book could not have been written
and our world would be a much darker place.

Contents

Acknowledgments

In order for this book to reach you, the reader, a number of people have contributed across the years in obvious and subtle ways. From this perspective, it truly is a collaborative work.

A debt of gratitude is owed to my family and relatives, particularly to Lea, Holly, and Melody for their encouragement, support, and patience living with a sometimes moody writer.

I extend thanks to Jeff, Mike, Marty, and Paul, fellow brothers and travelers on the Path, working together to realize potential.

Thanks to the staff at Llewellyn, particularly acquisitions editor Carrie Obry for recognizing this book's potential, bringing it forward into its present form, and for her personal patience.

Finally, a special thank you is extended to Melody and Kristen for believing, to Mollie and Lou for their generosity, and to Lea, for teaching me so many things.

Getting Ready for the Ride

During the days of your life, divine breezes will blow, so watch out for them.

—Mohammed

Journey of Opposites

Traveler: "O holy one, I have climbed mountains and traveled roads. I made my way through wind, rain, sun, and snow to find you. Now, please tell me, in order to sit at your side and find enlightenment, why must the road be winding and the journey so long?"

Master: "Before I answer your question, first you must answer one of mine. Do you agree to this?"

Traveler (hesitantly and with impatience in his voice): "Yes."

Master: "Very well, then, from all this going and doing—with its travels, opposites, and struggles— what have you learned?"

Traveler (pausing and considering several different answers before finally remembering one singular moment of clarity gained through watching the flame of an evening campfire): "One night, while contemplating and gazing into the fire, the thought occurred to me that while each day was filled with a variety of experiences, looking back at day's end these often chaotic and disparate events combined to form the day, and were all connected as part of my journey."

Master (with a smile on his face): "So now you are beginning to understand. Life, death, hardship, and joy are all part of the Path—opposites thrown upon themselves combining to form a tapestry, from which we learn, move forward, and reach higher."

For many readers, the title of this book will seem a juxtaposition of opposites—commuting and enlightenment—that couldn't possibly work together. Yet the contrasting images of commuting chaos and spiritual peace are designed to raise a question: can these two activities ever merge? That is the central premise of this book. As you read further, perhaps with a little guidance, you, like the student who gazed into the fire and found an answer, will see how commuting and enlightenment are entwined.

Unfamiliar Territory

Before starting our commute to work, we need to take a few minutes to discuss what might be unfamiliar territory for some travelers. This preparation will help you understand various points and sights along the way.

On one level, this book is about using our limitless human potential to make more from a troubling activity. On another, it is about commuting to work and applying simple meditation and concentration activities to make an ordinary and hostile situation work for us. In time, with training and preparation, this commuting activity becomes something more—an enjoyable spiritual journey.

This book has something to offer travelers from a variety of religious and spiritual backgrounds, and those searching for their own path—both commuters and non-commuters alike. In our complex and highly scheduled lives, often we do not have the time to take a few quiet minutes each day to contemplate and explore the many hidden parts of self. This is particularly true the closer we are to a large metropolitan center, rushing back and forth, traveling long distances to pick up our children and get to work on time. We will explore techniques to exercise and stretch our personal capacity while describing some of the conditions necessary to multitask in a careful, safe manner. Through examples and guided exercises, the reader is presented with different methods to access higher capacity and increased efficiency, both while working and while traveling.

Although all spiritual paths prescribe quiet time for personal development, some paths also teach that learning and illumination emerge from within the very fabric of active, daily life. We must remember that, within this context or framework, enlightenment occurs as an organic extension of a person's life. Enlightenment is a natural adding of spiritual capacity to balance and further enhance other capacities, with the outcome being personal excellence. Who says we all have to run off and become monks to find spiritual awareness? Traditions vary. Life is the great classroom, and we are all travelers on a journey. In our modern times, this journey includes traveling distances to work every day. What better place to test patience, help others, and make the world a little better?

Is It Really Possible?

A major question tackled by this book concerns the applicability of spiritual teachings to daily life. In a society that prides itself on outcome, often there is a healthy skepticism about the usefulness of spiritual values in an often hard, bottom-line, scientifically-oriented, and demanding modern world. In a newspaper article concerning the idea of attaining enlightenment while driving to work, one commuter hesitated and commented about his own experience of navigating stop-and-go traffic on the Tappan Zee Bridge in New York: "Why me? Why now? . . . It's never that romantic."

Is it really possible to make something more of an annoying, emotionally draining, and repetitive commute to work? Spiritual teachings assert that we all can reach higher under certain conditions and with a little preparation, and that it is possible to transcend daily activity. Often, it is a matter of attitude, training, and expectation.

This Method Was Perfected Millennia Ago

Throughout this book, I refer to the tradition of the Sufis and mystics. This path happens to be the way that I relate to my spiritual journey, but this wisdom is universal and can easily pertain to you. For those readers who have never heard of the Sufis, here is a short introduction about their viewpoint and words of wisdom:

- According to Sufi tradition, we all are on a journey traveling back to our Source, which is termed far, far away. We are on a cosmic commute of sorts, and have forgotten to use our spiritual capacity. This is the missing ingredient for many of us, and failing to develop and use this latent capacity has gotten most of us and society into trouble.

- Throughout this book, the designations *mystics* and *Sufis* are used interchangeably—and while my discussion in various sections about the Sufis will not answer all of your questions, it will provide a general orientation and, I hope, improve your journey. What is being added through this book and its traveling wisdom is a different perspective or way to look at your commute. What you do with this premise and opportunity is entirely up to you.

- At times, some of the references and sayings in this book may appear Christian and could confuse readers. According to tradition, Sufi perspective is consistent with all three monotheistic expressions, finding its most recent voice through Islam.

Background to the Guide

Next, a few words concerning situational background, the structure of the book, the Major Deegan Expressway, and something called discontinuous learning.

While this book is about making the commute to work something more, it is also about using the mind in a different way to overcome a tiresome activity. Because we are all products of our culture and environment, we have been conditioned to use our mind only in specific ways. These are the patterns, ideas, and thoughts our culture designated as important.

Yet other cultures teach different ways to use the mind. Consider the preparation of a child who grows up in New York City attending a private Catholic high school and the preparation of another who is schooled by Buddhist priests in Tibet. There will be similarities in thoughts and ideas, and also differences. Of interest to this discussion are the differences around the use of techniques such as meditation and prayer. Both of these children will be taught aspects of the same thing. Each will be instructed on how to get in touch with their spiritual center; however, the techniques and outcomes will vary considerably.

In the use of meditation, one child may be taught how to visually concentrate to free self from a tiresome, routine activity, while the other child may be given specific word groupings to communicate with their Source during Mass. In both situations, each child is learning to use their higher consciousness, but because of the focus there are different potential outcomes—with one activity being more useful on a daily commute than the other.

Millions commute to work every day. Some drive cars, some walk, others use bicycles, buses, airplanes, and trains. Some travel five minutes, others two hours. Some love their ride, others hate and endure it. One day I found myself using a meditative technique to free my mind from the drudgery of driving to work. It just sort of happened and came about naturally. This has helped me survive and transcend my daily journey on a monster of a highway: the Major Deegan Expressway.

The Deegan is only eight and a half miles long, but because of its linkage to key bridges and interstates, it quickly turns into a commuter's nightmare due to only slight weather changes or a minor fender-bender. As the highway winds its way through the northwest Bronx, 125,000 vehicles a day connect their drivers with many different corridors of life. As such, the Deegan plays an integral role in the economy and daily life of millions of people living in and around the New York City metropolitan area, which includes parts of New York state, New Jersey, and Connecticut.

Yet all large cities and towns have a heavily traveled major highway just like the Deegan; and as more and more drivers take to the roads, sitting in traffic has become an everyday reality for just about everyone.

While this highway was the route that I chose to get to work, I am certain most commuters, no matter how they travel, will see parts of themselves in the different stories and events in this book.

Next, a few words about the ride, the Sufi view of discontinuous learning, and the use of mile markers as chapter designations.

- This ride occurs over a period of months; there is no clear story line or sequence of events. This ride begins and things happen that may or may not be related. Then it ends. This is similar to the way we think and to some events we experience. Daily, we go about our business. The events of our day may not be joined in any obvious way. Then the day ends and we wonder at the meaning of it all. Yet from a distance the events are connected. They are part of our life and mind.

- Themes are presented, dropped, and picked up or restated later. Some learning happens this way. We need things repeated over and over, or presented in different ways to get the point.

Sometimes we may not understand an event until months or years have passed.

- Content and themes in this book are grouped using mile markers. Within this structure, material is at times organized with a singular thematic flow, and other times it is not. Mile-marker designations afford the opportunity to offer a wide and sometimes disparate range of material. These designations are numbered 1 to 8.5 and correspond with the length of the Major Deegan Expressway.

- This book is about a car ride to work, but the subject matter can apply to any commute or almost any activity. This ride is about learning from the most mundane of things. The Sufis maintain enlightenment can be attained in ordinary life, doing almost anything. What is required is a different way of looking at events.

Well, enough of getting you ready for the ride. May your travels through these pages be fun, educational, and filled with Light. Remember—don't limit the possibilities! Buckle your seatbelt and let's begin.

The Ride Begins

Though man originates from far away, is asleep and may return after he has attained the means, he can do so only if he works from a sound environmental base in the world in which we find him: our slogan is "Be in the World, but not of the World."

— Mevlevi Ustad Hilmi

The Ride and Personal Enlightenment

Last year, while I was on vacation in New Mexico, one of my friends there remarked, "You know, for someone who has spent most of his life in New York City, you're not as neurotic as some of the other easterners we meet. They're always in a rush and rude."

My friend continued, "A few weeks back, when I was visiting New York City and driving to the airport on the Major Deegan Expressway, I almost lost my mind. It was ninety degrees; the traffic was backed up. I had to open my windows and turn off the air conditioner. All around me were large trucks and buses. Exhaust was coming into my window, and I couldn't wait for the quiet of New Mexico. How can anyone find peace and not go crazy in that environment?"

I replied, "Over the last few years I have gone crazy at least a half dozen times."

When I returned to New York, I traveled to work along the same route my friend described. As I looked around and saw dirt, exhaust, and endless rows of vehicles, I realized something: over the years, I had learned to see beyond the Major Deegan Expressway. While part of me was busy driving the highway, another part was doing something else.

Sure, I got pissed off when the traffic was backed up at the approach to the George Washington Bridge and I was going to be late for work. Yet I learned to still this part of me, for the most part, and listen to that quiet, inner voice that sang of another realm and put things in perspective.

Millions commute to work daily. Once you've been at it a while, you learn ways to adjust. Depending upon their mode of transportation, commuters read, listen to the radio, share a conversation, eat breakfast, shave with an electric razor, fix their hair, order a drink, and curse their jobs.

Necessity teaches that we are many things, and that it is possible to do more than one task at a time. While traveling the highway, we see it every day. The Sufis have a saying, "The apparent is the bridge to the real." In part, what is meant by this is that we need things of the world to help us to experience, or see, the underlying

Unity. This reality is the Truth, or perception of the next world.

As I thought about the conversation with my friend in New Mexico and the difficulties of traveling the Major Deegan Expressway, I wondered if it was possible to attain enlightenment traveling to work every day. Particularly on a highway as crowded, dirty, and in need of repair as the Deegan?

Of course it was! A little unusual, perhaps, but anything is possible.

Gradual Building of Impacts

In some traditions, enlightenment is attained in one glorious moment of insight, which is transcendent and unifying. It is an experience that changes the course of the person's life. Most people seek to repeat this over and over—some with success, others not as successfully.

In other traditions, enlightenment is reached through a gradual building of impacts. These are smaller visions, or tastes of the Divine. This is a much slower process, but the goal is similar.

Mystic schools teach that each person is capable of learning to put aside the normal stream of consciousness in order to allow the Higher Self to emerge. In fact, this is the goal of the mystical process: stilling the world so the higher consciousness may operate. Once the student learns to quiet everyday thoughts so something else might happen, the student is ready to travel, alone.

During the course of the mystic's training, various exercises and tasks are prescribed. One of the most familiar of these is meditation, in which the worldly consciousness is quieted through use of a focus word, phrase, or point of visual concentration. By concentrating attention with a device (the focus word, a candle) and redirecting attention when it wanders, eventually the everyday mind quiets. In time, with this exercise and others, the higher consciousness emerges. It is a subtle essence, and our desires and daily thoughts often cloud our ability to perceive in this fashion.

Somehow, as I drove to work while focusing on the movements of the cars, trucks, and buses, my soul learned to sing. Part of me was busy trying to avoid the other cars, yet another part sang of its place in the cosmos. While my eyes focused on the road and my hands guided the wheel and shifted gears, my higher consciousness awoke.

Awakening to my higher consciousness was like listening to public radio—it had its own agenda and helped me realize, anew, that I am more than the guy who sweats and curses the building traffic.

Daily Journey

The symbol of a journey—the spiritual quest to completion—is an old one. Daily, we awaken with a multitude of possibilities; each morning we are reborn into a new life. Similarly, traveling the highway to work, the possibilities are endless.

While the pattern is similar—wake up, drive to work, work, drive home, do errands and chores, play—there are many possibilities depending upon our attitude. If we view the pattern of our lives as a repetitious set of responsibilities that has become tiresome, then we are limiting ourselves.

The task of the spiritual traveler is to see each day for what it is by focusing on the moment. When we are in the moment and free of our preconceptions, a host of possibilities become visible. These possibilities are like the variety of cars, trucks, and buses we encounter. The colors, styles, and shapes are endless; yet if we dismiss them by saying they are all vehicles, we are allowing our preconceptions to stop our capacity to be in the moment and see the variety.

In many ways, we create our own reality by adhering to certain thoughts, ideas, and fixed patterns. Freeing your mind of your old thoughts and fixing on the moment is how the journey to freedom begins.

The Deegan is not the only possible way for me to get to work. It is the way I choose to go. I feel it is the most direct route; however, often it is not the speediest because of its congested traffic patterns. In fact, I go home another way, because at 5:00 p.m. I feel there is less traffic on an alternate route. I am free to pick and choose.

Alternatives include driving through New York City streets or going part of the way on the Bronx River Parkway. I consistently choose the Deegan, because it suits me.

This pattern of choice and no choice due to fixed requirements in a situation is similar to many aspects of thought and behavior. We are all creatures of habit and ritual—some of which is helpful in structuring the day, and some of which is not.

What is important is that I get to work on time. How I get there, which highways I take, and my attitude toward traveling is up to me. Within each, there is a capacity to integrate all of life's events and view existence in a transcendent way. This capacity is the higher consciousness, and it exists along with our other skills, talents, and limitations. It is the part that knows where it is going; it knows the destination and the importance of the other parts.

Knowing the destination is often not enough to get you there. You must also know something about driving a car and which roads to take. Also, it is helpful to know weather conditions and traffic patterns; this knowledge helps ensure an expedient journey. All of the pieces fit together and are important in varying degrees.

Morning Drive and Repetition

My morning drive, while a long one of about forty-five miles, is filled with variety. It starts at 6:30 a.m. in the quiet tree-lined streets of upper Westchester County. Here one has to be careful to avoid both cars and deer. There are forested hills, miles of protected reservoirs, and construction crews widening the highways for miles at a time.

As I get closer to New York City, the traffic becomes heavier. I get on the Major Deegan Expressway in the northern Bronx. By this time I have traveled on four different highways—a distance of about thirty miles.

The Deegan borders the western part of the Bronx and, as it winds south, it feeds into the George Washington and Triborough bridges. When there is no traffic, I can make the trip in about fifty to sixty minutes. Usually, this is not the situation. Also, the later I start out, the more traffic I encounter. It often seems as if I am in an endless parking lot, waiting to inch forward.

Yet for millions this is nothing new or special. People do it every day, year after year. The task, as in life, is to make something out of the activity. In other cars, as you look about, you see people laughing with a radio show or talking with a passenger. Some are bored, others are smoking cigarettes. Each in their own way is trying to make the situation work.

———

The mystic claims that the pattern of repetition exists so that we can break free of it. It exists to provide struc-ture, and therefore it may be transcended.

Do not let me mislead you. My commute often is boring and repetitious. Many days I do not want to drive in the rain or snow. I would prefer to stay in bed or take the advice of the bumper sticker that reads, "A bad day fishing is better than a good day at work."

This is what life is like. Some days are better than others. Some commutes are easier, but you have to make do with what you are given. Often it is a matter of attitude.

Urban Crunch

You don't have to be a transportation guru to figure out that the closer you are to a city, the denser the traffic patterns will be, particularly around rush hour, and that your daily ride to work will potentially take longer.

In fact, if you live in a metropolitan area with a population of over 250,000, the United States Census Bureau reported in 2004 that you are more likely to spend nearly 30 minutes or more getting to work every day. Additionally, if you live in one of the five counties that comprise New York City, the figure is likely to be nearly 39 minutes per day. Nationally, Chicagoans come in second with an average time of 32.7 minutes spent commuting.

States with some of the longest commute times are New York (30.8 minutes), Maryland (30.0), New Jersey (28.3), Illinois (26.7), and California (26.6). All are above the national average of 24.4 minutes. States with the shortest commute times are North Dakota (14.8 minutes), South Dakota (15.0), Nebraska (16.1), and Montana (16.7).

While living near a large city increases travel time to work, big metro areas also have more transit choices available because of the density of people, which balances things out. Urban commuters can usually select between dependable public transportation (bus/train/subway), car services and cabs, walking, or even bicycling.

For people in rural areas, commuting is most often by private automobile, and reliable forms of mass transit are much harder to access.

No matter if you commute five or fifty minutes, the task in commuting, as well as in life, is to make the situation work for you. Even on a short run, traffic can back up, and you can become delayed and stressed out worrying that, for example, no one else will be at the office to cover the phones. Often in repetitive activities, minutes can stretch into an eternity; it is important to have a few tricks or relaxation techniques available to disarm the troubling thought patterns that come up in these situations.

A Variety of Landscapes

Some days it seems as if the highway is in chaos. Cars are darting in and out of lanes. Buses are cutting off trucks, so the bus drivers won't be blocked in a slow-moving lane. Cars are stalled, horns are blaring, and drivers are cursing each other.

Yet you drive a bit farther and, suddenly, everything is calm. Motorists keep to their lanes, the speed limit is being followed, and order is seemingly restored.

———

This is sort of the way I am. One minute I blow my top and think everything is lost. The next, the problem is solved and I am calm.

Always, there is a design; sometimes, I can't perceive it.

———

Trees sometimes grow in concrete. Wherever a little soil gathers, as nature wills, a seed will sprout. When you look at the dividers between the northbound and south-bound lanes, you see this miracle all around.

———

Occasionally, as you drive beneath highway overpasses, you see pigeons nesting. Somehow they have made their home amidst stone, steel, and exhaust fumes. The need to survive is strong... One creature's purgatory is another's home.

———

In many ways, I am the thoughts I think. While driving down the highway, my interpretations of what I see are based upon my previous experience.

Today, it was raining, and depending on if I like or dislike rain, I was affected in a particular way. Rain can be cleansing or a problem for driving. It can help to cause an accident or help flowers grow ... Rain is any number of things, and my response is usually based upon my pre-conceived ideas.

On a daily ride, how do I process all these different observations, thoughts, and repeating patterns? As you gaze about and see the world filled with seemingly end-less variety, you cannot help but wonder and struggle to make sense out of it all. This is our inner desire for order and purpose.

According to the mystic, the mind questions and is confused so that one day the heart might answer.

Night-Before List

In many ways, getting to work on time and spiritual studies are similar. Yet when rushing out of the house in the morning, one easily forgets that both the physical and the spiritual are connected, that each is an exten-sion of the other. On the ride to work in the morning, to experience our spiritual side it becomes easier if we are calm and have prepared for the ride and day ahead. This preparation sets a tone of intention, is personally nurturing, and helps care for our needs. When we are prepared, less distracted, and a little more centered, perhaps we may be in a position to help another traveler.

To get out of the house in the morning, many commuters prepare in part the night before. To them, such preparation makes common sense. If it fits your style, get a sheet of paper and list those things you can get ready in advance: select and lay out clothing, make lunch, set the alarm giving yourself extra time, take out the garbage, get gas for your car, recharge your cell phone, lay out different articles for the day's ride (business carry-all, clothes for the dry cleaners, shopping list for food on the way home), and listen to the next day's weather report.

———

In order to get to work, many things have to be in place. I have to get gas for the car, make my lunch, and set out my clothes the night before. To arrive at work on time, I need to be up by 5:45 a.m. and driving on the road by 6:30 a.m. Otherwise, the traffic is too heavy and I arrive sometime after 8:00 a.m., which results in my rushing before the 8:30 a.m meeting or walking in to it late.

This timing requires a discipline of sorts that has gotten easier over the years. Now it is second nature. Similarly, for the spiritual traveler's success, many things must be in place. There must be a correct interaction between student, teacher, and the Path. Also, the student must exert the right amount of discipline and do things in the correct order.

Seeing What Is in Front of You

When questioned about the definition of a Sufi or the end product of this form of learning, one of the great teachers of the Path replied, "To be a Sufi is to see what is in front of you."

It is a rare skill to see what is actually in front of you, as opposed to what your past experience and thought process indicate is present, or what others have taught and indoctrinated into you.

Mentally, we are extremely adept at categorizing and generalizing things, often instantly. This ability has been honed over millions of years and has helped the human race to survive. When we were hunters and struggled physically on a daily basis with many enemies, we needed to know and recognize instantly when a threat entered our environment. We needed to form an opinion instantly and react, based on limited information: a sound, a movement caught out of the corner of an eye, the sudden appearance of a strange animal or person in an open field.

In today's complex world, the threats are not often as physically imminent, and the use of this skill has shifted into other areas. We all want things simple, and our natural ability to generalize quickly makes complex, modern life more manageable. It helps us know what we like and dislike. Also, if we broke down every decision or thought pattern into all the positives and negatives, we would never take action and eventually get bogged down.

However, as I have seen on my daily commute, reacting instantly to events by generalizing can be troublesome and can limit my potential, depending upon when

I use this ability, if it is applied accurately, and whether I am even aware that I am doing it.

When questioned about their daily commutes, most people think commuting is a pain, and they feel they have no choice in the matter. However, while this belief is part of the daily reality for millions of commuters, it is not the only possibility. As I have experienced it, the daily commute can be much more than just drudgery, and to see what is actually in front of you takes a certain mental posture or frame of mind. Fortunately, this more positive way of viewing things can be learned and, according to some, is the singular indicator of an enlightened person.

Seeing reality, as opposed to what I have categorized into a neat compartment based on past experiences, is a very helpful skill in my everyday life. Seeing what is actually there, as opposed to what I have inserted into the situation, allows me a wider range of options and happier, more tranquil thought patterns. With this flexibility of thought, you can also gain greater freedom to express who you are and eventually unlock your spiritual capacity.

Seeing What Is in Front of You Exercise

At a day's end, make yourself comfortable. Take a long, hot shower to wash away the day's negative energy. Put on some comfortable clothing, sit in your favorite room, and slowly take in everything you see. See all of the different items: furniture, pictures on the wall, knick-knacks, books, and electronics. See all these items together that you have selected to be part of your life. Observe their collective color and feel their pleasing energy. After looking around the entire room, feel yourself going deeper into a relaxing frame of mind. Feel the tension leaving your body. Give yourself an inner suggestion to relax even deeper, as you sit amidst all your favorite possessions. After you have looked around the entire room for a minute, take another long, deep breath and tell yourself to move on to the next part of this exercise.

Next, visually inspect an individual piece of furniture very, very, slowly. See your favorite piece, your easy chair, sofa, or bed. Visually trace and inspect the curve of its construction. With your eyes, slowly follow the outline and flow of the entire piece. Inspect the texture of the supporting material and what physically makes up its form, structure, and slope. Describe the piece of furniture out loud—its motion and construction; how you obtained it; its color, shape, and size. Notice the empty spaces between its legs and arms, and the breadth of its openness and expanse.

Next, indicate what you like about this piece and how it has helped you. Be as detailed in your description as you can be. When you have finished with one piece of furniture, move on to the next piece, and then on to other items in the room. For variety on successive days, start with different categories of items. One day begin with your knick-knacks and the next day with your books.

Do this visual detailing and individual inspection daily for three to five minutes total. Repeat this exercise for five days.

How This Exercise Will Help

Over time, this exercise will help you to see things individually instead of instantly categorizing them into overly tidy groups. I noted earlier that when we categorize, we have the tendency to oversimplify, to take things for granted without recognizing individual items and their potential. It is as if you were to see all travelers as commuters and make a decision not to speak with any of them because you consider it too much of a bother, or as if you categorized all bus rides as annoying. Instead, recognize that some days a bus ride can be more enjoyable and less crowded, and that there may be days when you even want to share your experience by striking up a conversation with a fellow traveler.

— THOUGHTS FOR THE ROAD —

- You have been given enough for the journey.

- Number the wonders of this realm. Do you believe the worlds to come will be any less majestic? The road is a long one—but O, the many riches!

Signs, Learning, and Life

The object of Sufi spiritual teaching can be expressed as: to help to refine the individual's consciousness so that it may reach the Radiances of Truth, from which one is cut off by ordinary activities of the world.

—Idries Shah

Highway Signs

As we travel the highway, we see countless signs. Some announce an exit, that it is time to leave the highway. Others depict a bend in the road or an upcoming hazard. These signs have been posted so that travelers can arrive at their destinations in the speediest, most efficient manner. On the spiritual path, the teacher assists the student by showing them how to read different signs. In this way, the student, another sort of traveler, might one day continue the journey on their own.

Sometimes signs are obvious, and sometimes they are subtle. On most highways, the obvious signs are those that tell you when to exit, or when there is an approaching division in the highway. On the Deegan, these signs are the typical green-and-white variety.

Yet you would be in deep trouble if these were the only signs you were anticipating. You also have to observe directional lights and the brake lights of the cars in front of you. Drivers change lanes as if they were in a race. You also have to look out for drivers who don't use their signals. Here, things are trickier. As a driver, you anticipate moves because of an emerging pattern. Sometimes you can pick up a move by the shift of a driver's head or a wheel beginning to turn. A rule for safety is that you should never change lanes without anticipating that someone else will try and outrace you for the spot.

Spiritual signs are rarely as dramatic as those of the highway variety. Throughout our days, learning opportunities rush past us like the air at fifty miles per hour, often unnoticed. Somehow, we must learn to slow down and make more use of the experiences all around us. In the spiritual journey, most signs are hidden or very quiet, yet people expect changes to be announced by a host of angels. It doesn't happen like that. The organ of perception works when other things (your desires) are still; that is intuitive insight.

At times, the higher consciousness is a special knowing, but often it is only a matter of understanding the pattern that is forming. If you have seen a pattern before, you are pretty sure how it will turn out.

———

The best traffic reports are generated by those radio stations that have helicopters to patrol the skies. As you drive to work, you see them circling a trouble spot and you begin to play closer attention to the radio, hoping to avoid the area.

The saints of God monitor spiritual conditions in a variety of ways. They do so through reports of others, through firsthand experiences, and sometimes they do so by reflecting the Light to different individuals. Through the higher perception, they know what is going on and they act or don't act, depending on the situation and design.

Like a radio, the higher consciousness can send you messages that something is about to occur. It is almost like a traffic report—when the report comes on you know to watch out for something. Most often, it is general awareness, or an internal warning, that something requiring extra attention will be occurring. Accompanying this awareness is a surge of energy to help you succeed.

Chain of Humanity

At night while driving home, I am reminded of my place in the community—one traveler in the endless chain of humanity. Ahead of me, I see the tail lights of twenty cars; behind me, in the rear-view mirror, I see the lights of twelve more.

As I journey home, the light that has been aglow in my heart continues to illuminate my way.

Spiritual Experience

Last night my wife said to me, "With all the noise in this house, the only place I can find peace and quiet is my car. There I'm able to turn off the radio, be with my thoughts, and center myself. For those moments, it's a real spiritual experience…"

This was unsolicited. I just looked and listened.

Carpool

If you've ever been part of a carpool and shared the responsibility of driving to work, you realize there are pros and cons to this arrangement. For example, while it is good to have company on a routine ride, sometimes you want to be by yourself with your own thoughts as company.

On the spiritual path, we must seek Truth both as an individual and as part of our community.

The potential for a positive experience increases dramatically when the individuals involved are in harmony.

Getting Out of the House Checklist

One commuter told me that before she leaves her house every day, she likes to have everything in order. For example, she makes sure the dishes are washed, the garbage is taken out, and everything is picked up and put away. All this preparation, whether she does it the night before or in the morning, gets her mind ready for her commute and for work. The activity and routine helps prepare her to use relaxation techniques should the commute get nasty. When she gets home in the evening, she also knows everything will be in its place. That knowledge makes her feel comfortable.

If a listing-and-planning exercise fits your commuting style, create a checklist of things you need to do before leaving home each morning. Set your alarm a few minutes early so you do not have to rush, and as you go along check off each item, either on paper or in your mind, until these duties become second nature. Examples may include: walking the dog, waking up/dressing/ feeding the kids, bringing the newspaper inside, checking the weather report, checking travel and road conditions, making sure your front door is locked, and taking the kids and their assorted belongings to the sitter or to school.

Discipline, the capacity to plan and follow through, to complete a score of routine items, is useful for daily life, work, and commuting. Interestingly enough, these same personality characteristics are an essential element to spiritual studies. However, in the spiritual endeavor it is grace and Divine Blessing that truly are the miraculous parts.

Learning and the Complete Life

Back on the highway, heading toward work, it feels good
to be healthy, joining in the commerce of the city. The
complete life is one in which both the spiritual and the
physical realities are joined. We were created to participate in our community, yet retain the capacity to see the
world from another vantage point. This view is integra-
tive. "Be in the world, but not of it."

We were not all created to live in caves as hermits and
contemplate our navels. Who would travel the Deegan
into the city so that worldly affairs might prosper?

———————

During the course of the day, there are many opportunities to embrace the Truth. When viewed in a certain
manner, the smallest event can be the instrument for
teaching and enlightenment. Most days are filled with
routine tasks that are part of the process of caring for
ourselves and others. Driving to work, fixing dinner, or
making phone calls are examples of this process.

Yet when the mind is tuned to the higher consciousness, it is possible that these events will become something more. In order for this to occur, there must be a certain alignment between person and event. This alignment only comes about after a period of preparation.

You might ask: "Why should I get involved with all of this? It sounds like some mumbo jumbo you made up not to go crazy driving to work." Spiritual learning is your birthright. Humanity is evolving into a higher condition. This is part of the Plan. Unless things change, we as a race may never reach beyond our current state. Unless we start to use our higher consciousness, we will never be able to think of others and act in our own best interest. We will be doomed to repeat the mistakes of the past. This perception is the balancing factor, enabling us to do things we thought impossible.

———

For the spiritual traveler, the soul is described as traveling upward toward completion. Its stay in this world is one stage in this process. Every day we awake with another opportunity to find fulfillment, live our dreams, and take part in our community.

Commuting to work is similar. Every day we travel to fulfill obligations and take an active part in the world. Our success in both endeavors is related to training, natural ability, our attitude toward the process, and destiny or luck.

We are born to participate in the everyday affairs of our community, yet we keep a part of ourselves detached and sacred. As we participate in the world and focus our attention on our jobs, another part of us is in harmony with the Light. This is the part that cannot be touched by the world and is transcendent.

———

Some people see cars as an extension of their identity, connecting with the world. They must have a vehicle of a specific year, color, and model. They feel that this represents who they are. Others drive as if they were in a Grand Prix or NASCAR race, weaving in and out of traffic just to arrive a few minutes earlier. Neither of these things is either good or bad; they are a matter of effect. How does the need for a specific type of car influence other aspects of our lives? Will driving like we're in a race result in a traffic violation or lead to injury?

In both situations, these external manifestations are linked to internal conditions. The driver sees himself in his car and the way he drives; on an inner level, he *is* the race-car driver and the car.

Once the inner focus is awakened and we are not concerned to the same degree with externals, our choices become greater. We do not have to have this thing or that, but we may choose to drive in a particular way. After we learn who we really are, we can choose to do or be any number of things.

Things We Hate

As a teenager I remember saying to myself, "What a waste of time commuting and taking part in the world this way." Living next to the Cross Bronx Expressway, I saw thousands of cars daily make the drive to and from

New Jersey. I vowed to never put myself in that position and to live as close to work as possible.

As the years passed, I moved my family to the suburbs. I, too, joined the seemingly endless flow of commuters. This was something I hated to do. I felt I would lose part of myself, driving to work every day. And as I grew older, there were other things I didn't want to do, but that I had to do. Some were far more difficult than driving forty-five miles to work every day.

Gradually I realized that, because of the outcome, sometimes we have to do things we hate or don't want to do. I commute to work because of the benefit I get from it: we live in the suburbs and I can be in the city as well.

In spiritual studies, the rule is similar. Because of the desired outcome, you have to do things you don't want to do. You must give of yourself so that something else might happen.

Background Information

Many things about commuting are straightforward and repetitious. People quickly adjust in order to set up a routine that conserves time and energy. We are all creatures of habit and rely on these comfort cycles to function in the world. Yet there is another part of us that yearns for adventure and new experience. This is the part that can look at the mundane, crack a joke, and then be free—joy riding on laughter.

Commuting is a relatively new phenomenon, and daily we are stretching the limits of how far and how fast we travel to work. According to one source, the term *commute* is derived from the reduced or "commuted" fee paid by the purchaser of a season rail ticket. In this instance, a lesser amount is paid in advance for a ticket that covers journeys for a period into the future.

Commuting habits are constantly changing and depend on a variety of personal, financial, climatic, and situational factors. Obvious influences include the location of the job, the worker's proximity to a large metropolitan area, and the cost and availability of transit options.

Due to increasing costs, more and more businesses are opting to have employees work from home. This practice has become so prevalent that the word *telecommuting* was coined to describe it. Telecommuting usually involves forwarding work and staying in contact with the office electronically. As an added convenience, many colleges and schools are offering online courses. It seems that just about everyone agrees with the dictum "Don't commute unless you have to."

For great numbers of people, obviously, the option of working at home does not exist. Depending upon your proximity to a metropolitan area and where you have to travel within it, your transit choices might include buses, trains, a car, a vanpool or carpool, a bicycle, or your own two feet. Whether you are a passenger or a driver during your commute will determine if you have time for yourself or if you must focus instead on ever-changing traffic patterns.

As I indicated earlier, my interest with this book is to add a spiritual dimension to the commute. Obviously I can't get you out of the traffic, but I may be able to help you, depending upon your inclination, to sing along with the music of the Universe.

As William Blake, one of my favorite poets, proclaims in the poem "Auguries of Innocence," it is not the quantity but the quality of an experience that is its measure, for there is vision and higher potential offered in every moment. Blake writes, "To see a world in a grain of sand and a heaven in a wild flower, hold infinity in the palm of your hand and eternity in an hour."

Personal Choices

Although some of my neighbors commute by bus and train, my choices are more limited. The hospital where I work is not easily accessible by either bus or train; it is situated on a small island in the East River, adjacent to Manhattan. I drive to make things work for me; it is the most direct route and taking the bus or train doubles the length of my commute.

Yet I know people who travel by bus nearly ninety miles to their jobs, a trip that averages two and a half hours both going and coming. Fortunately, they can kick back, let someone else drive, and go to sleep. With almost five hours at their disposal every day, they also have the option to sleep, read, listen to music on their iPods, converse with fellow travelers, watch the scenery, work on their laptops, study, or call home on their cell phones and check on things.

Every step of the way provides the opportunity to begin a new journey, every commute a potential to awake and connect with your Higher Self.

More Highway Signs and Memories

Life's highway is filled with countless signs, mile markers, memories, and exits. As I travel down the Deegan, gazing at the diversity of the city landscape, my soul celebrates and calls out.

Watching the sun rise over Yonkers Raceway as the trotters take their exercise; seeing the endless variety of trucks, cars, and buses heading toward the city; feeling the birth of a new day, with its millions of possibilities—all of it makes me glad to be alive.

How to live this day? What to do? What to accomplish?

Try to make one person's life a little easier, a little more complete. Help rather than hurt. That is the prescription for a useful life and day!

———

Nearer to the George Washington Bridge are the old apartment buildings where I lived first when I was born and later in my early twenties. As my mother told the story, when I first came home from the hospital I was so small that I could sleep in a furniture drawer.

Over time this area has changed. From my old apartment, the view of the river has been obliterated by a larger apartment house. The open, grassy spaces around the highway have been filled in with concrete, garbage, and even newer buildings. Nothing remains static.

Sometimes changes are not for the best. The wheel of life continues and our only hope is to rise higher, becoming truer to our lasting self.

It is true that I am not the same person who lived in those buildings years ago. Yet part of me *is* the same; this is the part that will guide me into the next world. This is the part that sings as I travel the Deegan.

————

On top of a hill in upper Manhattan sits George Washington High School, my old alma mater. How I hated high school! I drive past the school daily on my way to work. Sometimes I think about the good and bad times of those years. I enjoyed playing handball on the school team, but I can't recall much else I liked about the place.

As the years passed, I came to realize I enjoyed learning, but I often disliked the repetitious formality of school. Later I came to see school as a preparation for life and for learning, the center of life.

————

There is another bridge called the Washington Bridge, different from the George Washington Bridge that connects New Jersey and upper Manhattan. The Washington Bridge connects the Bronx and 181st Street in Manhattan; from the Deegan, it looks like part of the entrance ramps to the larger George Washington Bridge.

As a youngster, I would walk with my brothers across the Washington Bridge to our grandparents' apartment on Undercliff Avenue, adjacent to the Deegan. Driving under this bridge every day, I am reminded of my youth and of my grandparents' love and excitement when greeting us. Truly, those were good times.

The Washington Bridge has recently been undergoing rehabilitation—some painting and cleaning of rust. The old bridge must be made useful for modern times. It is the same with spiritual teachings. These teachings, or bridges between the physical and spiritual realms, must be tuned up for today's world, and presented in a form that is accessible.

Thought Monitoring

Throughout this book, I will note the importance of monitoring your individual thoughts—in this case, in connection with a daily commute to work. For students who have been in a spiritual school, thought monitoring and the recognition of individual patterns of consciousness are some of the first things they learn. In doing so, the student learns about the repeating nature of everyday consciousness and how certain thoughts can be disarmed through substitution activity. That is, in part, what meditation teaches: how to substitute a pleasant focus word or visual image for a repeating and sometimes irksome thought pattern.

This is a good skill to have on the ride to work. When the traffic is backed up and I'm going to be late, it is essential that I monitor my reactions and minimize the time I might spend in a negative zone. To control my thoughts, I use a short focus word or mantra that I like. I repeat it slowly, over and over in my mind. On the ride to work, I use this word whenever something happens or the traffic backs up. After I react emotionally to the event, in time I usually calm down by slowly repeating the word and concentrating each time, over and over.

Many people use as their focus word a name or concept from their religious background, such as *Jesus*, *Mohammed*, *Allah*, *Love*, *Light*, or *Vishnu*. Others use whatever personally pleasurable relaxing names or visual images they like, such as *sunshine*, *happiness*, or the name of their spouse or lover. I repeat one of the names of God and visualize light and healing energy attached to it. Feeling this energy emanating from this glorious name heals and soothes me.

For further instruction on using your focus word during meditation, refer to the deep-breathing exercises beginning on page 193. These exercises combine the use of breathing, Light, and a focus word. Besides helping you to relax, they will lift you higher.

Thought-Monitoring Exercise

At the end of the day after you have taken care of all your chores, select a quiet, comfortable place to review your thoughts about the day's commute. Before beginning this review, you may wish to take a long, hot, relaxing shower to wash away the day's events.

Next, sit down and relax in your quiet place. Take several deep breaths very slowly. Have a pen and a blank sheet of paper handy. Sit quietly for approximately thirty seconds and think about the day's commute and ride home. As you recall your journey, write down two things, people, or occurrences during your commute that troubled you. Write down your thoughts and reactions. Next, write down and list two things, people, or occurrences that you enjoyed. Also write down your reactions to these and why they were pleasing.

Finally, write about how you would change or modify the situation or your reaction if you could be given another opportunity. Slowly repeat this corrective action to yourself twice. Repeat the entire exercise daily during the next three days.

How This Exercise Will Help

By practicing this activity, you will begin to recognize troubling thoughts that occur on your commute. After a time, you will recognize that some thoughts repeat themselves and are potentially destructive to your mood and well-being. Also, by practicing this exercise you will have identified thoughts that are pleasing, and that you can substitute during your commute when something unpleasant happens. Make your substitution thoughts, ideas, and words as simple as possible. The fewer words, the better. A mantra or substitution phrase is usually very short; the best ones are limited to one word.

— THOUGHTS FOR THE ROAD —

- That which is formless takes on a physical shape so we may know it.

- Just as water must undergo change to become snow, so must we undergo a process of alteration. Slowly, the world of the senses must be taught to give way to the world of the soul—then the change is complete.

MILE

3

Happiness and Everyday Experience

Imagination blocks you like a bolt on a door.
Burn that bar.

—Rumi

Making a Situation Work

In the midst of writing this book, I began to wonder what purpose it will serve. Then it occurred to me that much of our lives is spent doing things we don't like to do but have to do, many of which are dull and repetitive. Driving the Deegan is a symbol for anything we do that becomes something we would choose not to do, but that we must complete out of necessity or duty. If we have exerted as much energy as possible to make a situation work for us and yet we cannot change it and are still unhappy, what is left for us to do? Change our attitude, or somehow find a way to benefit.

In reality, I can only control the traffic I face by so much, by varying my travel times. The Deegan gets lots of traffic at all hours. Yet I have some control over myself and my attitude toward commuting. Over time I realized that the best approach was one of quiet acceptance, and doing those things that help me deal with the situation. I could listen to the radio or travel with a companion. However, the best attitude for me was one of neutrality and acceptance. More often that not, traffic is backed up. That is an unavoidable reality.

Once I became aware that the only thing I could control was myself (and that even my ability to do that was subject to fluctuation in mood), other things began to happen through an acceptance of my daily commute. I began to listen to the quiet, deeply hidden part of myself that saw the world in a unifying pattern. This part of me accepted that I had to travel this highway every day, something another part of me hated. The higher part taught me that I could make something of the situation if I was open to the possibility.

We all have tasks in our lives that we hate to do. Some people have options and are able to replace these tasks with others. For some this isn't always possible; part of the function of this book is to offer an alternative way of viewing that which we dislike doing.

You ask, "How do I acquire this alternative view of quiet acceptance?" This view is an aspect of higher consciousness, and is acquired through (1) practice going inward; (2) learning from who and what is around you (remember that just about any experience can teach you something about consciousness, people, and situations); (3) preparing how to learn by recognizing thoughts, expectations, and patterns that stand in your way; (4) using exercises and techniques that help remove obstacles (thought processes) that block your progress; and (5) following the direction of one who has accomplished all of this already.

In this journey there is a traditional guideline that helps clarify an important aspect in the process of spiritual realization: often it is not a matter of adding something, but rather of removing that which blocks your way. This awareness is already inside of us; the traveler's task is to learn how to recognize and temporarily remove that which keeps their higher awareness from coming forward.

The capacity to view the ordinary as something extraordinary is not a static condition. It comes and goes. Sometimes my journey through the Bronx is a long, tiresome ride. However, at other times in my commute, I am tuning in to another portion of my consciousness and my journey is much more meaningful.

Spiritual Evolution

We are indebted to and connected with those who came before us. Millions of people have worked on perfecting the automobile over the decades. Even before the idea of an automobile was a possibility, items like wheels, engines, and carriages had to be invented. Consider for a moment all those who helped perfect these useful, necessary items.

The roads we travel took years to plan, build, and pave. How many trees were torn down? How many people had their homes moved? The engineers who designed the roads were educated by those who had engineering knowledge before them, and who passed it on for centuries in classes, books, and journals.

Consider the modern machinery that needed to be invented so that we can drive to work, machinery that pulverizes stone and helps move mountains. Consider the bridges we cross. Who conceived them? Who helped build them? Who discovered and perfected the process to make steel? I think you get the idea. We are connected in so many hidden ways to the past and to those who came before.

Humanity is continually evolving toward something higher. Each of us is a link in the chain that extends far into the past and reaches into the future. Part of our destiny is to awaken the higher consciousness; the method to do so, perfected millennia ago, is available today. One day this path will be as common as waking up, getting in your car, and driving to work. Today this possibility is a potential about to bud.

Importance

Each of us has an exaggerated view of our own importance. By nature we are self-centered, but healthy adults try to redirect toward others, at least in part, this concern for their own needs. A little self-centeredness is good; too much can be destructive.

This morning when I went outside to start the car at 6:30 a.m., I was faced with a flat tire. By the time I filled the tire with the contents of an inflator can (a marvelous invention), got the tire repaired, and purchased another inflator can, I had lost three hours. Somehow the world did just fine without me during those hours, although I worried the entire time.

The mechanic who fixed the tire told me the rim was bent. Probably one of those potholes on the Deegan got me. Sooner or later, we are all victims of the potholes of life. Perhaps in part they exist to test our view of our own importance?

Hard Work

One of the bridges that connects Manhattan and the Bronx is the 207th Street Bridge. Going south on the Deegan, the Fordham Road exit leads to this bridge.

When I was in high school, I would take the subway to 207th Street in Manhattan, walk across this bridge, and play handball on courts that are still located alongside the Deegan. These were my high school's home courts, and they continue to be maintained by the New York City Department of Parks and Recreation.

I was captain of the handball team for two years. In those days we were the doormats of the league; I think we only won one match in two years. It was embarrassing and often discouraging to lose so much.

By the time I was a senior, I had figured out that it took a great deal of hard work to be a successful singles player. While our team lost most matches, our first singles player was excellent and usually won his games. I played second singles and won half of my games. However, we needed another victory from either the third singles player or one of the two doubles teams to win a match. These victories were difficult to come by.

In order to be successful at something, you need talent and plenty of hard work. But often talent and hard work are not enough; you need the right combination of other factors as well.

In spiritual studies, an interplay of factors is essential for success; it must be the right time in the right place with the right people.

Our handball team was not successful, since not all of the players wanted to work as hard as was necessary. Often we asked the third singles player and four doubles players to practice longer and harder, but they had other priorities and obligations.

In order for the spiritual traveler to succeed, there must be an interplay between the teaching, the teacher, and the student. Hard work and discipline is a given. The magical piece is the grace of the Path, which pulls all of these factors together.

Flexibility

I rarely drive home on the Deegan, for two reasons. First, at 5:00 p.m. the traffic patterns are terrible near the approaches to the George Washington Bridge. Second, two nights per week I work late in New Rochelle, a small city well to the east of the Deegan.

Over the years I've learned to listen to the traffic reports, and I've experimented with every route imaginable. This flexibility is necessary for me to get the job done, to get home in the shortest amount of time.

In higher studies, the teacher should be able to teach in any format, and be flexible enough to present the teaching in a way the student will understand.

Sometimes a religious framework is used. Sometimes a psychological or scientific framework is used, or a self-help book about commuting. It depends upon the time and place.

Happiness

The other night during dinner, my daughter asked me, "Are you happy in your new job?" I replied, "Why do you ask?" She said, "Each night when you come home you don't look very happy." I answered, "I like my new job, but it tires me out and the commute home takes a while to get out of my system. It takes a few hours to distance myself from the day's events and traffic."

I tried to answer her question as simply as I could. Perhaps another day we can take the discussion further. Happiness is a state of mind, and for the most part it comes and goes. It is also a state that can be learned and refined. We often make ourselves unhappy by replaying those things that we consider distasteful.

When something happens that is painful, it is usually over in a matter of seconds. We all have a tendency to extend a painful event by talking about or remembering different aspects of it. While getting something out of our system by discussing and remembering it is helpful to a certain degree, most of us do it far too much.

We all need to recognize our patterns of negative thinking so that we can consciously make the decision to be happier. If we are aware of our "old demons" and know how to disarm them, we can replace them with happier, more tranquil states.

And it is only after we become masters of our psychological processes that the spiritual awareness matures and comes more easily forward.

Happiness Tips

For most of us, our main source of personal happiness is the little things we look forward to in life. Sure, big events like a new car, the birth of a child, or a marriage are sources of great celebration. But for most people significant events such as these occur infrequently.

It is the little things we enjoy daily that consistently enrich our lives. Seeing friends or grandchildren, having that first cup of coffee in the morning, or watching our favorite show on television—for most people these are the ingredients of a happy life and day.

In order to further enjoy the daily commute to work, I encourage you to create a "happiness calendar" of the little things that you can anticipate and add daily to your ride.

Examples on my calendar have included: packing something good to eat or drink, getting an audio book or music CD at the library to listen to, setting the radio to a new station, and bringing along for the ride a different flavor of coffee or candy. As a passenger, I've added to my calendar a phone call I need to make to a friend or loved one. For some company on a long ride, I've been made happier by driving with a co-worker or neighbor.

———————

Our spiritual consciousness is part of our capacity to experience the world. It is one mode of consciousness among others.

When trained to do so, we are able to tune into this part of ourselves—just as we might tune in to the radio as we drive—and operate through this level of awareness.

For some, tuning in like that is as natural as finding a radio station on a car's FM dial—the buttons are already set to the station, the preparation has been completed. Indeed, this holistic, enabling mode of consciousness is part of us. Our task is to learn how to wake up to it and use it.

On the highway I have witnessed accidents and I have seen the face of death. One afternoon while I was driving north on the Deegan, just below the approach to the George Washington Bridge, I saw the immediate aftermath of a multi-vehicle accident involving a car and an 18-wheeler. Somehow the front of the car wedged itself beneath the rear of the truck. This was not a pretty sight; a passenger in the car had his head crushed beneath the rear of the truck, and the rescue squads had not yet begun to dislodge him. This accident victim looked younger than me, but his time had passed. The look of his still body, his head twisted and lifeless, has remained with me.

While I am in this world, my task is to make the most of this opportunity. These precious moments of life are my challenge to do positive things.

We come into this realm and then leave it—all to what purpose? For some, this remains an imponderable riddle; for others, the answer is clear.

To learn and serve. Ultimately, we are here to learn and to serve. This is the teaching.

> *Happiness is rooted in misery. Misery lurks beneath happiness.*

> —Lao Tsu

Quick Shifts

To bend like a reed in the summer rain and dry in the warmth of the afternoon sun—that is the challenge life affords. So much of commuting and daily experience demands a quick shift in consciousness. How do we consistently choose more positive, more nurturing, and happier states? One method is to remember what the wise have taught us. Misery and happiness are part of the same fabric and follow each other.

———

Another Monday morning. I wonder how many more times I will travel this route to work. It could be a hundred, a thousand, or never again.

No one is promised another day.

———

Daily, I take the Taconic State Parkway to the Sprain Brook Parkway, before traveling on Route 100 for about two miles. Next I get onto the New York State Thruway, which becomes the Major Deegan Expressway. The Deegan feeds into Randall's Island and Ward's Island.

One Path. Many names. This is the way it has always been.

———

Creatures of habit. Waking at the same time, driving to work by 7:30 a.m. A patterned existence—all part of the natural tendency toward repetition. O, how we resist the urge to break free and embrace our joyous, transcendent nature!

Only in those rare moments of intuitive insight do we break the physical chains, crash the barriers of the ways we think and act.

Traveling the same route to work, coming home by a fixed hour—repetition leads you to the door; intuition sets you free to pass through it.

———————

Driving past Van Cortlandt Park, I am reminded of how much I enjoyed, as a boy, playing in those open, green spaces. A park is a haven from the noise and daily routine of urban life. It is a place to enjoy and refresh ourselves so that we might continue with our lives.

Within each soul, there is also a place that is quiet and special. When we retreat to this center on a daily basis, we come forward more complete and able to serve.

This is our seat of power, our oasis amidst the routine of daily life.

———

So often my morning drive is affected by my state of mind. Am I worried about work and distracted? Is one of my children sick, or does one of them need extra money for a bathing suit? These worries affect my capacity to be in the moment and accept what is before me.

How to be in the present, surrendering to the situation? How to experience what is actually present, without carrying our own baggage? This is only learned through the grace of the Path.

When I find myself being distracted, I turn inward and draw strength from that which is transcendent. Then I am in harmony, able to accept and see what is before me.

Learning from Everyday Experience

The wise claim that we can learn from any situation, person, or object. In this respect, anything or anyone can be our teacher. In order for this learning to occur, an attitude of openness about learning from different situations is required.

As I have indicated, the daily commute can be a complex teacher, instructing us about ourselves, others, and the world in which we live. For example, consider how bumping your head upon entering your car teaches you to bend lower and take your time getting in and out.

As commuters, do we all need a thump on our head to go deeper within ourselves? While commuting to work, is it really possible to gain useful insights about ourselves and others that will help us in our daily lives? Of course it is. All it takes is willingness and instruction.

Try the following self-observation exercise to learn more about yourself. This exercise is a companion to the thought-monitoring exercise in the last chapter. By adding a step, this new exercise takes the practice further and deeper.

End-of-Day Contemplation and Writing Exercise

This lesson is designed to build on the previous exercise and to help you identify learning lessons that occur on your commute.

Make yourself comfortable, and take a long, hot shower to wash away the negative energy of the day. Put on some comfortable clothing and find a quiet place to sit and contemplate the day's commute.

Slowly visualize yourself beginning the commute, traveling and arriving at your destination. Along the way, consider the different people you met or saw, the scenery you passed, and the things that caught your attention. Recall the landscape—see it in your mind's eye and consider the obstacles you encountered or something that made you laugh and become happy.

Next, recall from your consciousness two events that happened or two thoughts you had during your commute that have remained in your mind. Consider why these two events left their imprint on your awareness. Write the reasons down. Now go further and ask yourself what these events or interactions taught you. Write the learning lessons down and consider their importance to you. Stay with this for approximately sixty seconds.

Finally, say a prayer or offer up a suggestion to your Higher Self that will free you from negative, repeating thought patterns, and that will incorporate the intended learning lesson into your life. For example, use something like this: "O Lord (or O Higher Self), help free me from today's inner entanglements, and help me to use these learning lessons in a positive and helpful way." Sit quietly for thirty seconds.

How This Exercise Will Help

Over a period of time, you will begin to recognize how life is the great classroom, as well as recognize what types of events leave an impression on your awareness. By identifying learning experiences and noteworthy thoughts and experiences, and by using individual prayer and suggestion, in time you will recognize the spiritual or higher potential in events.

- The canvas is the world. You are the artist. Pick up the brush. Create your own life.

- The hardest battles are not fought in fields or on distant seas, but within ourselves. We are the enemy who ravages every defenseless position.

Opening the Door

Look on the world as a bubble. Look on it as a mirage. The King of Death never finds him who views the world like that.

—The Buddha

No matter how magnificent the total work of this world, one day it must change, eventually passing into dust. History teaches that this is the way of all cities and civilizations. So much effort. So much beauty. To what effect is all this?

I am reminded of the Buddhist monks who create elaborate sand paintings with beautiful designs and colors. These take weeks to create, and many people work on them. Usually there is a specific design to begin the work, and the interplay of colors and patterns is extraordinary. Yet when the work is completed, it is immediately destroyed.

The purpose of it all is in the living, and only a life that is aligned with a higher goal is complete.

In the Moment

Some mornings, the monotony of the drive and the routine of working each day makes me weary. I begin thinking about all my problems, and I am trapped. This is the snare of yesterday and of expectation; it is no longer living in the moment.

When I am one with the moment, I am able to soar free. Part of my mind fixes on the routine and repetition of the drive; another part is able to sing the song of freedom.

The problems of yesterday and the expectation of the day's events are jailers. They are yesterday's reality and possibility for today. They are not the moment. Only by living in the moment can I begin to operate beyond the confines of time and space.

Boundaries

There is a sign that hangs over the Deegan announcing that drivers are entering New York City. One moment you are in Yonkers and the next in New York City; you have crossed the boundary line. I remember when I would get excited about crossing into New York City, my home. This was years ago, when I traveled home on weekends from Rochester.

For many reasons, borders are drawn between municipalities, and these borders are essential to the way we operate our governments. We are all familiar with this kind of boundary. More subtle boundaries that have a greater effect on our lives are the boundaries in our minds. These invisible lines often do not allow us to see beyond past experiences—they are limitations created by our own capacities and by institutions within society. These boundaries help create the way we think and operate.

To break free of these patterns is truly liberating. One way we can accomplish this is through higher perception, gradually acquired through the use of concentration exercises such as living in the moment.

When you are focusing, concentrating, and in the moment, you are seeing what *is* present, not what you *think* is present. The higher consciousness is always there; we have simply put a wall around it with our patterned, conditioned thoughts.

Danger Rocks

Up along the left-hand side of Route 100, as it feeds into the New York State Thruway, is a cluster of sharply cut rocks. They rise about seventy-five feet from the road and at their crest is a fence to protect walkers from falling down the slope. These rocks stretch nearly a mile.

When I was younger, my brothers and I would play on rocks similar to these. We called them "Danger Rocks," because you had to climb over a posted fence to get to them. The sign on the fence read "Danger" in big bold letters.

Yet the fun of the adventure was the danger; you could get injured, or caught by the park attendant. If he found us in this forbidden zone, we knew he would tell our parents.

I have not thought about the Danger Rocks in years. I wonder what I have replaced them with? Perhaps the adventure of self-discovery?

Island of Dreams

Sometimes when I am caught in stop-and-go traffic, I feel like I'm in a cage. I can't wait for the traffic to open up and to be free of the entanglement.

It is similar with the soul; it too is trapped and longs for its home among the stars. When set free, the soul sings a song of triumphant splendor.

Your body is the car, the events of your life are the entanglements, and your soul is the driver.

Within each one, there is a magical place. As you learn to re-enter it, it becomes more familiar. It is an island of a million possibilities. Every day I learn to use it more and more.

All along the drive to work, I see different worlds. These are nothing compared to the island of my dreams.

Congestion List

For those of you new to commuting by car or who need a little coaxing to get better organized, this section will help you when the inevitable occurs—when the traffic is backed up, and you are stuck a distance from the nearest exit. Perhaps you haven't learned the alternate routes to your destination, or you are a little nervous about experimenting with a new route while everyone at work is waiting for you?

A good commuting strategy is to develop a fun and practical set of activities to do while you are stuck in traffic. This list of activities is a complement to your commuting happiness calendar, and it may include some of the same items—such as listening to a favorite CD, calling someone on your cell phone, singing along with the radio, or munching on a snack.

After you have taken all practical measures to either get out of traffic, or after you have called the office to let them know you are delayed, sit back and enjoy something from your list that is healthy for you. Here are a few practical tips on what to do when you encounter an extended stop-and-go situation:

- First, monitor traffic stations to determine the nature and extent of the backup.

- If it is an extended delay, consider getting off the highway and taking an alternate route. If necessary, pull over and consult a map or computerized direction finder to determine an alternate route.

- Make phone calls to your office or child-care provider to let them know you are being delayed.

- If you cannot get out of traffic, sit back and give yourself a mental suggestion to relax and enjoy the delay by trying one of the various strategies or fun techniques you have planned.

- If you become tired and frustrated, exit the highway and go to a restroom, or get something to eat or drink. Or pull over to the side of the road, get out of your vehicle, and stretch your muscles. Remember that until you are ready to continue, you can always wait out some or all of the delay.

- When you get to work and have time, question other people who drive the same route about alternate routes they use to try and beat traffic. Or get a good local map, showing all the local roads. Keep this map in your glove compartment until you need it.

Discarded Treasures

My grandfather lived for many years on Undercliff Avenue, which borders the Deegan just north of the Washington Bridge. In those days, there was still plenty of grass around the highway, as well as underdeveloped land between the highway and the Harlem River.

My brothers and I played in those open spaces, looking for discarded items. People sometimes dumped things in the open lots. Or a passerby on the highway would throw an item out their car window. We were always looking for something special. We usually found coins, balls, and old pens and pencils. These were treasures to us.

In the world of higher studies, undesired experiences often turn out to be vehicles for growth. How many times have we learned a lesson by experiencing something distasteful or by having a setback?

Airport Parking, Planes, and Commuting

Just as we may become confused and lost in an airport parking lot, so too may we lose our way on the spiritual path.

Only with the guidance from one who has traveled this way before is the traveler protected from this pitfall.

The most direct way is the Golden Path.

———

The wise claim that the impact of an event is never singular. When something happens, the effects are multi-layered. Take the example of a plane crash. Everyone would agree that a plane crash is a terrible tragedy and scores of lives are changed forever. Yet the impact of this event does not end with the families involved. If you look closer, you will see other effects.

The hospitals where the injured are treated are affected; a clean-up and rescue effort is begun immediately; investigations are started to examine causes; manufacturers may be sued for faulty material; insurance companies pay or reject claims; families anxiously await news of loved ones; people are frightened and refuse to fly; and scores of lives are altered by injuries and deaths.

As this multilayered impact exists with events, so too does it with an individual's life. The impact or importance is never singular. We are unable to count the levels.

———————

The other day I was waiting for a flight at a mid-sized airport in the southeastern United States. As I sat in the boarding area, a businessman sat across from me, dressed in a white shirt, tie, and dark suit. He was clearly taking the same flight as I was; as we all waited to begin boarding, he was making routine follow-up calls to different customers in a somewhat loud voice. As he continued speaking, it became clear that every week he made this flight of hundreds of miles, to follow up with and serve his customers.

The more he spoke, appearing focused and meaningfully engaged, the more I wondered how this book could help him. He was using the extra time waiting for the plane to board to take care of business details. He was putting his time to good use and he didn't seem to need anything further. Later, as the day and his commute became tiresome and slowed to a halt, he might grow antsy and require a different outlook. Then he might profit from an enlightenment strategy. Should he require it, one can hope a copy of this book finds its way to him.

Rubbernecking

Rubbernecking is a term traffic reporters use to describe motorists who slow down to look at a stopped vehicle or accident. Passing motorists turn their heads, often twisting their necks to get a better view.

At first I thought this phenomenon was attributable solely to the "Thank God it's not me" relief people feel. Later I began to realize that is part of it, but the reason goes deeper. It's about safety. Our biological instincts make us react to something that is potentially dangerous. We could have been injured, or we could have had mechanical problems. Our system goes on alert status, and we are compelled to respond by looking.

This instinct for survival operates in everyone and manifests on a spiritual level. As a result of feelings of emptiness and lack of direction, we feel something is wrong.

Heed this reaction. It is a natural warning.

————————

Why do news reports accentuate spectacular tragedies and often ignore the less dramatic ones?

You see, there is something in us that dates far into our past. When humans were hunters, in order to survive we had to be keenly aware of that which was unusual in our environment. If a dangerous animal approached, our senses had to instantly be aware of it. In a manner of speaking, our biological history draws us to the unusual or dramatic. We are easily excited so we can survive.

It is important for us to understand this fact about ourselves and others, so that we won't be controlled by this instinctual need. This is of particular importance in the area of higher studies. Many people are drawn to this teaching or that one because they find stimulation or excitement in it. The question they should ask instead is: does this teaching work and will I benefit from it?

Worrying

People create problems for themselves so they will have to struggle. While the worldly consciousness is occupied with these affairs, the higher consciousness lies dormant.

In order for the higher consciousness to operate, the worldly concerns must be pushed aside. Through prayer and meditation, practice pushing aside worldly concerns daily, and as God wills, one day you will awaken to find this mode of consciousness is as normal as the other.

Do not be afraid! You are the door that stands in your way. Go beyond fear, and you will find peace and awareness in the ocean of the Beloved's Love.

Morris Heights Train Station

Parts of our lives are spent waiting like passengers at a train station. Some pass the time by studying the people around them. Others engage in conversation or sleep. Some busy themselves with the schedule, while others consider the mechanics of the engine and cars.

Rare is the individual who can grasp the workings of an entire transportation system and how it is created by the collective energy of thousands of people over hundreds of years. Rare is the individual who can describe how the system serves as a source of social, political, and economic activity for a region or nation.

Rarer still is the individual who can foresee a disaster and intervene by altering factors and harmonizing their effects. This view of the function of things and the capacity to modify factors is called by some the higher consciousness. It is the birthright of humanity, and it is available if you search for it and are taught to use it.

Power Plant on the Hudson

Religion is like an old power plant that has fallen into disuse. During its time, the building served to fill the countryside with light. Now its doors are closed, the windows broken, and the machinery still.

Periodically, an engineer arrives to rehabilitate the structure. The engineer has the expertise to direct the workers and update the building to today's specifications. Then the engines start anew, creating light for thousands of homes.

Our Potential

All around us are examples of wonderful scientific advances and technologies. New hospitals, expansion bridges, fuel-injected engines—all declare humanity's capacity to control the physical environment and increase the span of life.

To what purpose will the extra years we gain be put? Will we be doing the same activity, like commuting, over and over again? Or will we reach higher and travel the Golden Path to spiritual enlightenment?

Two Things at a Time

Some will wonder how it is possible to free the higher consciousness while driving a car. How can you do more than one thing at a time? Isn't it dangerous? Don't you need your full attention on driving?

Yet we are always doing more than one thing. Our brain is simultaneously controlling a variety of physical and psychological processes.

On one level, the higher consciousness is just one of the many functions of the brain. All mystics maintain that both sets of consciousness can coexist. It is natural and the result of training—nothing more.

Yes, it is possible to drive your car down the highway, and instead of singing along with your favorite song on the radio, sing along with the rhythm of the Universe.

Highbridge Pool

On the western side of the Harlem River, just south of the Washington Bridge, is Highbridge Park. When I was growing up in Washington Heights in upper Manhattan, my mother often took us to the Highbridge Pool. This was the only way to beat the summer's heat. Hundreds of people waited in line for hours to go swimming.

Once inside, the clear, cool water provided welcome relief. We stayed there all day, splashing and enjoying ourselves.

In some ways, religion is like the clear water of yesterday. A place to return to and come forward, refreshed to face the day.

Yankee Stadium

In all things, there is an element of the Divine. Driving past Yankee Stadium, which is located adjacent to the Deegan, I wonder how baseball is a reflection of the unseen world. As my mind begins to work, numerous parallels emerge:

- The ball represents opportunity and the bat our capacity to direct action.

- A team must work together in order to be successful; similarly, many faculties or abilities are required to lead a complete life.

- Each player is given a number of opportunities at bat, just as each of us is given a number of chances to try something.

- The game is played for a fixed period; innings represent stages in one's life.

- Although a game, baseball is taken seriously by many people. In order to be successful at anything, an attitude of seriousness is required.

- Ultimately, this form of endeavor is a pastime, something to occupy us until the next phase or activity requiring attention.

- On the team, each position requires many skills—some similar, some different. All positions are important. Each of us during the course of our lives assumes different roles.

- During the baseball season, if you lose a game, there is another chance to try and succeed. In life, there are numerous attempts and opportunities. Many believe there are other realms with multiple wonders awaiting the soul.

My First Deer

This morning on my way to work I hit my first deer. The poor creature jumped out into the middle of the Taconic, while cars were whipping along at sixty-plus miles per hour. I swerved to avoid the animal and she twisted to miss me, but I clipped her in the head with my front bumper.

Watching the doe fall, through my rear-view mirror, I saw other cars steering to avoid the struggling creature. Luckily, no one else was injured.

Strangely enough, this all happened at 9:30 a.m. Usually, you have to watch out for deer at dusk, at night, or in the early morning. Not at 9:30 a.m. when everything is bright and sunny.

I had slept late, because I worked the night before and was anticipating a leisurely ride to work. Not so. After the deer incident, I had to brake and swerve around three other cars at various times.

Each time, by just inches, I avoided serious injury and damage to my car. No one else was injured except for the poor animal.

How fragile the line between life and death. One moment we are here—the next, someplace else.

A Fuel Spill

Last week there was a fuel spill on the Deegan that necessitated closing the highway. Fortunately, I heard about it in the traffic reports and turned off the highway by the ramps to the George Washington Bridge. If I had gone another half mile on the Deegan, I would have been caught in that mess; some of my colleagues were delayed three hours before they arrived at work.

Interestingly enough, it wasn't until the second traffic report that I made my decision to exit the highway. I was nervous about whether or not I could adjust to a new route through Manhattan. Would the new route change result in time saved or just added frustration?

For me, everything worked. I figured out how to get to the Harlem River Drive from upper Manhattan and entered Randall's/Ward's Island from the Manhattan approach to the Triborough Bridge.

Sometimes you know what to do, but are afraid and worried about the outcome. It isn't until circumstances reach a certain level that change is an absolute necessity.

With higher studies, the principles are similar. While people may have an interest in learning something new or changing an aspect of themselves, it isn't until they must take action because of individual circumstances that change occurs.

More about the Deegan

I went to the Major Deegan Expressway webpage and found out more information about the highway:

- The Deegan is 8.5 miles long.

- According to the New York City Department of Transportation, 125,000 vehicles travel the road daily. That's more than 45.6 million vehicles per year!

- The Deegan was constructed from 1935 to 1956— a period of over 21 years.

- The highway is a major connecting thoroughfare for the Northeast Corridor, winding through the western Bronx and feeding into the George Washington and Triborough bridges.

- In 2005, a major rehabilitation project on the forty bridges that cross the Deegan was completed at a cost of $426 million.

- The highway is six lanes wide—three lanes traveling in each direction, north and south.

- The Deegan is part of Interstate 87, and a continuation of the New York State Thruway.

Tolls and Costs

Randall's Island leads to Ward's Island. Every day I pay a toll to get onto Randall's Island.

Fortunately, there is no toll for leaving the island; we are not charged for this privilege.

In everything there is a cost, whether it is time or money. Some costs are hidden and others more obvious.

Before you begin an endeavor, it is wise to determine if you have enough resources to reach the destination.

In higher studies, travelers are able to determine this only by the burning in their hearts.

You Are the Door

For many travelers on a spiritual path, meditation is a familiar technique. In the next chapter, Mile 5, a form of visual meditation and concentration is offered as one method for overcoming and transcending the daily ride to work. In this meditation activity, travelers still a part of themselves so consciousness more tranquil and more enjoyable will come forward.

Essentially, the traveler, while meditating and concentrating, is quieting and pushing aside the door of noisy or troubling thoughts, using a focus word or concentration point to redirect consciousness; and over time, with practice, another level of awareness is set free. When thoughts stray, the meditator redirects thought back to the focus word or concentration point, without emotion or worry of failure. In time, this redirecting process gradually "quiets" distractions, and another part of consciousness is unlocked and comes forward.

This emerging aspect is peaceful, tranquil, and integrating. In time, through repetition and practice, this technique becomes easier and the traveler enters or unlocks this level of awareness, seemingly at will.

In discussing meditation, two pieces of information need to be offered. First, meditation is one form of spiritual exercise, and any organized program of development includes a variety of experiences, exercises, materials to read, and individual prescriptions. Under the teacher's direction, these all come together to help develop a more complete traveler.

Second is a caution about the overuse of exercises— there is a human tendency toward overdoing useful techniques and something called "spiritual greed." Because meditation and concentration have so many positive effects, one must be cautious about the basic tendency to self-prescribe, about assuming that "the more I do, the better it will become." Remember to use your common sense; too much of anything can cause a disruption in balance.

You Are the Door Exercise

As with earlier exercises, make yourself comfortable. Take a long, hot shower to wash away the day's negative energy. Put on loose-fitting clothing and go to your relaxing, quiet spot to rest and turn inward. Before you begin this exercise, select a Name of God from your personal belief system. If you don't have a personal belief system, select a pleasing focus word or image, such as *sunshine, rose,* or *peaceful stream.* Make yourself comfortable and close your eyes.

When you are ready, imagine yourself coming home from work to a two-story house, tired and unsettled. You open the door to your home, and when you get inside you realize your dwelling is very quiet. You are the only one home.

As you gaze around, you begin to feel an irresistible pull; something is calling you to walk upstairs. You feel energy pulling you forward, and you realize that to deny this energy would be to deny part of yourself. As you climb the steps to the second floor, you are a little nervous. There is a flutter of anticipation in your belly. You are not sure what you will find.

There are sixteen steps, and as you slowly ascend them you grow more excited and nervous. Suddenly you find yourself praying and, for no conscious reason, repeating the Name of God (or focus word). Somehow, repeating this Name makes you feel safe, and you repeat it slowly, over and over. Then you realize that you are being called to one of the bedrooms, located at the top of the stairs.

As you repeat the Name and feel this irresistible pull, you realize your home somehow feels different, as if you were seeing it for the first time. You are standing outside the bedroom and the door is closed. You realize what has been calling you is on the other side, and you are no longer afraid. Calling the Name has made you strong and peaceful. Without effort, you open the door and walk inside the bedroom.

Wonderfully, the room is filled with brilliant, soft, blue and white light. Silently, this light embraces you and fills you with peace and joy; as you experience this joyful spiritual caress, you realize this light is your home. As the light continues to fill and embrace you, it instantly heals you, and you forget about everything else. Taking a seat on the floor, you sit quietly—filled with peace, joy, light, healing. You are connected to all living things. You realize this energy, which is emanating from you and is part of you, is the same energy that is in everything. Here you continue to sit for five minutes, at peace, connected to all things, but these moments linger, seemingly stretching into eternity. Repeat this exercise daily for three days.

How This Exercise Will Help

In time, this exercise will help you experience your own spiritual center, connect you with your Higher Self, and push aside the door of everyday awareness, which is blocking your way.

Divine Friction

Together the Master and traveler sat, eyes closed, meditating on the Light. How long they sat this way is impossible to say, and as the Master reflected the Light upon the traveler's heart, slowly the traveler became a small sun unto himself—emitting loving, peaceful healing energy.

Through the Master's guidance, the traveler was connected at his spiritual heart with the Light of the Universe; through a spiritual caress, the traveler had become One with all things. Now, as a drop in the universal sea of love, he danced with eternity, aware of both his own individuality and the inner connection to everything around him.

Master (clapping his hands, calling to the traveler): "Now, awake from the slumber that has been your life and ask me the questions that fill your mind!"

Traveler (slowly opening his eyes, trying to acclimate to the world of forms): "Master, I know you have spoken about the meaning of opposites many times, and how on a deep, inner level they are really connected, combining to form the fabric of our lives. Yet I am still confused. Why must life be a series of ups and downs, happiness and sadness? Why can't life be a singular joyful experience of the Light? Why is the world created both as a source of great joy and sadness?"

Master: "The world is a multilevel expression of the Light. At their center, as you have just experienced, all things are connected and One;

and once you have sipped of this Unity, your heart is joyful and triumphant—having tasted its home. Yet even with this proof, mind continues to question, for that is part of its job.

Remember that darkness and light, joy and pain, work together by creating a friction or resistance, sometimes clashing in upon themselves. This resistance, or unease, propels the traveler forward, always seeking and questioning—until the day when the traveler experiences the singular, connecting, glorious spiritual Unity and answer.

As one of the Servants of God has said, 'Gazing at the earth from the moon, all things—human wants and desires— are lost in the Oneness of this magnificent, multicolored orb as it travels through the heavens.'"

As the traveler sat and considered the Master's reply, he realized anew that in this journey mind asks the question, and heart ultimately answers it.

— THOUGHTS FOR THE ROAD —

- You are the door that blocks your way. Open it. Experience another part of yourself.

- Everything you have ever wanted or dreamed of is waiting within. All you need is the key. Pick it up! It, too, is within reach.

Way of the Heart

Whoever is initiated by us and follows us and loves us, whether he is near or far, wherever he is, even if he is in the East and we are in the West, we nourish from the stream of love and give him light in his daily life.

—Bahaudin Naqshband

Is it possible, really possible, to do more than one thing while driving? Of course it is! We see it all the time, but give it no thought. As I noted earlier, people listen to their radio, have conversations with passengers, worry about their problems, and dream up wonderful solutions to these problems while driving their cars.

We begin to limit our own capacities and possibilities when we believe something is not possible. With the correct preparation and practice, why can't someone experience another dimension of their mind while driving a car? This be accomplished using a simple meditative technique. Throughout this book, I have been discussing using your mind in another way while driving to work. This ability is accomplished through a gradual preparation, and this preparation includes using a visual meditative technique while driving your car.

For those who are unfamiliar with meditation and have never tried it, familiarize yourself with this exercise over a period of time, and at first use it sparingly while driving. Also, I would suggest that you first try using this simple technique under stress-free driving conditions. If you are going someplace for the first time and are worrying about getting there safely, save the exercise for another time. This is how I do this exercise:

- I focus lightly on the license plate of the car ahead of me and begin silently repeating my focus word.

- As I begin to relax and find my consciousness starting to expand, the higher consciousness awakens.

- If I am distracted by driving conditions, I refocus using the technique described above when conditions are again safe.

I have been at this many years, and for me this technique is natural and easy to accomplish. If you have never tried meditation or have little experience with it, let me refer you to Herbert Benson, MD, who has scientifically validated the benefits of transcendental meditation (as if it needed it) and has written two excellent books that will help you become familiar with the practice. This is the technique Benson has outlined for practicing meditation:

Step one: Pick a focus word, phrase, image, or short prayer from your personal belief system. (Examples include Jesus, God, Buddha, Yahweh, and so on.)

Step two: Sit quietly in a comfortable position.

Step three: Close your eyes. If you are driving, focus lightly on the license plate of the car ahead of you.

Step four: Relax your muscles.

Step five: Breathe slowly, naturally, and repeat your focus word(s).

Step six: Assume a passive attitude. When you find your mind wandering, gently return to the repetition.

Step seven: Continue this process for ten to twenty minutes.

Step eight: Practice the technique once or twice daily.

If you are driving, remember to use this technique only under stress-free conditions.

> *Choosing is the emptying of the heart of all things other than the search for completion. This resembles a visualization that the body is empty, and all thoughts have left it for a moment, during which time the true thoughts flood in.*

—Al-Hujwiri

Living in the Moment

Living in the moment is a mystical state in which the normal faculties of consciousness are suspended. The ego, or I, recedes and the higher consciousness comes forward. In this condition of surrender, one is free of preconceptions, intellectual baggage, and desires. It is a state of acceptance of what is transpiring, awareness of the unifying mechanisms in events, and intuitive perception. This is not a static condition, and it is not maintained throughout the day. After training, this state may be triggered by the focus word or other devices.

How does this highly technical, somewhat ambiguous description relate to driving on the Deegan? When I find myself becoming overly anxious, annoyed, or distracted by negative thoughts, I enter this state of consciousness. The end result is that I become more fully integrated and able to accomplish what needs to be done. Accompanying this state of mind is another level of energy and capabilities. If you have ever driven on the Deegan, or a highway like it, you know how helpful this state of mind can be.

Potential to Reach Higher

Suppose you were driving along and suddenly discovered you could not shift into third gear. The clutch engaged sometimes, but other times it didn't. After a while, this would begin to affect the way you drove. You would get into the right-hand lane and only pull out into the center when you had successfully made the shift. You would become tentative and, at the very least, you'd be delayed by this problem.

On some levels, this is the condition of humanity. We are on a journey, without all the capabilities of a vehicle operating at full potential.

Without the higher consciousness, our lives become a potential that is only partially used.

Bird of the Soul

How many people would believe wild pheasants live in Manhattan? Well, not exactly Manhattan but Ward's Island—which is in the East River just several hundred feet from Manhattan, with a Manhattan mailing address.

Not many people would consider this a possibility. Most stereotypes of New York City involve a large city full of concrete and steel, with multiple problems and millions of people. No one thinks about a wild game bird surviving in an urban environment. Yet these birds exist, and their pheasant ancestors must have lived on the island for centuries. Pheasants can fly, but they can't fly long distances.

Once again, our minds limit the possibilities . . .

Under the right conditions, the drive to work can become a wondrous journey of beauty and surprise. Under the right conditions, the bird of the soul can fly free.

Light in the Darkness

Near 161st Street, on the eastern side of the Deegan, the Lighthouse for the Blind runs one of their larger programs. They own a number of buildings. On the top of the tallest building beckons a small lighthouse approximately fifteen feet high. This symbol of hope and light in the darkness honors those who cannot see.

Within each soul there is a longing. This is our Light to illuminate the way home, and when it is aglow it is our beacon for the dark night.

We Are What We Think

More and more work is being published on the importance of positive thinking for a good attitude and good health. The more I read, the more I am convinced that we are what we think.

Clearly, many factors influence our thoughts—and many of these influences are outside our sphere of control. Yet how we react to things, in large measure, is a matter of conditioning, and is something that can be changed.

We don't need behaviorists to tell us that it isn't good to worry all day or that negative self-image affects career potential. What we do need are many different people, many educators, and many systems that help maximize our capacities to think positively and productively use what we have.

Some would argue that this is the realm of psychologists, and that is true to a point. However, many cultures have systems that help develop human potential. We in our scientific frame of reference have, until recently, scorned the usefulness of these tools and systems.

Fortunately, Western scientists are beginning to re-evaluate their initial dismissal, and there is a reawakening of age-old knowledge to harness the power of our minds, bodies, and world(s).

The *New York Daily News* used to run a series of sayings by Confucius, and one has always stayed with me: "A happy man thinks happy thoughts." This is true. However, what is missing is how to get to the point of thinking happy thoughts, or how to correct situations in which only unhappy thoughts are generated.

Humanity has struggled with this problem since the beginning, but there has always been an answer: turn inward and embrace your Higher Self. Until recently, we were looking in the wrong place.

So, when you are driving your car and the traffic builds up and you start to lament your "outcast fate," turn inward. There is a positive, uplifting station waiting to be played.

Many Selves

Robert Ornstein, PhD, suggests that the human personality is made up of many parts and smaller selves. We are a composite of parts, some of which are inborn and some of which are developed by situations and potentials.

From my point of view, the task of the spiritual traveler is to get to know these many selves. Identify them and be aware of their operation, so that over a period of training you can learn to still them. Once stilled, we can begin to listen to other parts of self that only operate under this condition. Stilling something is much different than obliterating it, the premise being that the higher consciousness can work within the normal personality. We don't have to change all our smaller selves—only modify some of them. Then the lasting self will come forward.

Just as I play with the radio while driving the Deegan, looking for a song I like, so have I learned to play the radio stations of my mind.

Advertising Myths

Ultimately, a car is a form of transportation and nothing more. Yet in our culture cars are status symbols and extensions of our personalities.

How did this come about? It was a story we were told through advertisements, and a need to express our individuality.

Is it possible that we have done the same thing with our religions? Of course not! That couldn't possibly have happened . . . or could it?

Khidr—Green Bringer of Light

Driving in from Westchester County, the closer you get to New York City, the less green you see. Gradually, trees and shrubs are replaced by asphalt and buildings.

In some traditions, green represents the higher consciousness or Light. The mystic guide of the Sufis, Khidr, is called the Green One. He travels the earth mysteriously, intervening according to Divine Plan, doing good works and dissipating spiritual darkness.

While God is everywhere and present in each heart, under some conditions the communication is strained. On one level, the city represents those things that get in the way. Yet as you look closer, you will see parks, gardens, trees, and shrubs throughout most urban areas.

God is always present. We are the ones who forget, getting caught up in the asphalt and concrete.

Reflecting the Light

The Light is the binding force of the Universe. It is the mother and father of us all. For *Star Wars* fans, it's akin to the Force that Luke Skywalker learns to use.

It is an enabling and enriching element; without its presence we would dry up and wither. The Sufis are the guardians of the Light, and they reflect this element into each portion of the world daily.

Some days, as I drive down the highway to work, I reflect the Light to those I love and care about. Using my heart as a mirror, I am one of thousands reflecting the Light of Eternity.

The Way of the Heart

According to Sufi tradition, we all have an aspect of the Divine within us. This spiritual center is comprised of spiritual fabric most like God (the Light), and is located in our soul. Because this center is termed "the heart," travelers on this spiritual Path have at times been called followers of the Way of the Heart.

On this Path, as I learned from my teacher, the job of the traveler is to wipe away the "dust" that covers the heart. In this way, the heart might become a clear mirror to reflect the Divine Light; this "dust" is an accumulation and has been caused by years of selfish living. The traveler's task is to wipe clean the mirror's surface. This is accomplished by an interaction between the student, the Master, and the Path. The point of all this activity is to create a completed human being—a person who reaches toward human excellence by using all capacities and is a mirror for the Divine Light.

Early on in our training along the mystical Path, students were taught to take the Light as it originated from God and entered this world, and then reflect it out across our hearts to those people we loved and were concerned about. In this way, through our purposeful direction for those we cared about, the Light would become an enriching and enabling element. Also, in time this Light would help wipe clean the mirror of our hearts, and we could participate in helping make this world a brighter place.

Practice the following exercise, so as you travel the highways to work, in time you too can reflect the Light and help dissipate darkness.

Heart As Mirror Exercise

Take a hot, relaxing shower and wash away the residue from the day's activities. Clean and refresh yourself, then put on loose, comfortably fitting clothing and go to your quiet place. Make yourself comfortable. Sit quietly and begin to focus inward.

As your mind wanders, slowly repeat your focus word and request God's help with this activity. Turn inward and go deeper. When you are completely still, free of distracting thoughts, imagine your spiritual heart, located near your physical heart, as a mirror. See this heart/mirror and feel its vibrancy and inner life. This is your home, your spiritual energy center.

Next, in your mind's eye take your hand and imagine yourself wiping away the dust that covers your heart. One strong stroke to wipe clean the surface. If your mind wanders, slowly repeat your focus word. Do not get angry with yourself. Turn inward, go deeper, and return to your heart.

Next, in your mind's eye see and feel the Light of the Universe entering into this world. See it gliding across your heart/mirror and being directed out toward those you love and care about. Take this Light, pull it toward you, and reflect it out to others. See and identify each of the people you wish to caress with the Light. Feel the Light's healing energy and see it chasing away each individual's darkness, enriching their lives. Continue reflecting the Light for two to three minutes.

Repeat this exercise nightly for five nights.

*Like a car in rush-hour traffic, the soul is waiting
to break free. Imprisoned by its circumstances, the
soul longs for its home beyond the stars.*

Clearing the Dust

Even on the clearest of days, I can see a brown haze of
dust and pollutants surrounding the buildings as I drive
toward the city. Slowly, we are cutting off our supply of
oxygen. Admittedly, the haze has not been as thick over
the last few years. However, it is still ever-present and it
affects us in many ways.

To me, this is an outward representation of our inner
condition. Because we are not perfect, our thoughts and
actions often remain clouded.

Ultimately, we are the ones who stand in our own
way, creating an internal haze of unclear thinking.
Daily, we must remember to polish the mirror of our
heart, clearing the dust and rising higher.

Duty and Responsibility

Driving on the Deegan, I am reminded of the time as a youth that I promised myself never to live the life of a commuter.

Now, thirty years later, I have joined the endless row of humanity traveling the highways to work. Duty to my family and our desire for a suburban life have led me to become something I never wanted.

You know, it's not so bad. In fact, it seems natural. One spiritual rule describes this phenomenon: "To attain you have to give up the things you want and accept those you don't." This is done to free the traveler of desire, to teach the traveler about responsibility and assist them in reaching a place of acceptance.

Acceptance, or surrender, is neutral, and the higher consciousness operates under this condition.

How Many Dinosaurs?

Gasoline is made from crude oil, which comes from decaying plants and animals. I wonder how many dinosaurs it took to feed my gas tank over the past seventeen years so I could get to work? I guess if the dinosaurs hadn't died out, I'd be walking to work instead of driving ninety miles a day.

I don't know if I should be grateful or not.

The Heart Chooses

Driving down the highway, you see all kinds of vehicles. Some are brightly colored, others are dull and rusted. Some are made in Japan and some in the United States. Each is in motion, taking the traveler to their destination. Yet in the long run some work better than others. Some are superior in design and will be better maintained.

It is the same with spiritual paths. Each claims to take the traveler to their destination; all are equivalent in that respect. But there the similarity ends.

———

Then how do you know which path to choose? Use the same criteria you have been given to select a car. However, add one more thing.

When you pick a car, ultimately it comes down to what suits you and your circumstances. If you have little money to spend, you will pick a car that is the best buy for your budget. Or, depending upon your personality, you may pick any "old thing" as long as it runs.

In the selection of paths, there is another element—and that is sincerity or burning in the heart. Depending upon how honestly you seek, burning only for truth, truth will seek you. For some travelers, the Path chooses them; they are unaware of their own inner merit and yearn for a glimpse of their Beloved.

It is tradition that these are the ones who attain.

- Brief is our stay in this realm. Yet as we disconnect from our higher nature, these hours seem like an eternity.

- The teaching is discontinuous. Yet we expect to unfold at a given time, in a specific place, and at a regular frequency. This is the learning to which we have become accustomed.

MILE

6

States of Mind

There are a thousand forms of mind.

—Rumi

Consciousness is a series of shifting patterns that repeat over time. These repeating patterns of thoughts, stimuli, and emotions fall into four major groups. Most of our consciousness is comprised of conditioned thought patterns, stimuli from biological processes, and expression of numerous emotions. All three of these functions can operate simultaneously. The spiritual consciousness only operates when the other three dimensions are stilled.

We have learned to use only part of our mind and often in patterned ways. Most people have never experienced the fourth area, spiritual consciousness. Accessing it requires specific training and practice. The closest approximation is the artist's intuitive representations of reality.

Biological Processes

Our brain monitors numerous biological and physiological processes. Much of this monitoring takes place at a level that is below our ordinary consciousness; we are unaware of this monitoring and directing function. Usually when something is wrong or an emergency occurs, this monitoring activity jumps into our consciousness. Ouch, I cut myself! Or, I bumped into a chair!

Emotional Processes

Emotions are felt throughout the mind and body. Research indicates that emotions have a biological as well as a conscious component. There is a difference between tears of joy and tears of sorrow. Emotionally, we all are aware of this; biologically, science has proven that something different happens when we cry from sorrow as opposed to laugh from happiness. Emotions register in the brain and body and can override our intellect.

Intellect

We use our brains and consciousness to figure things out. This is the part of the brain that most educational institutions work with. We use our intellect to reason, plan, add, subtract, and so on. Our schools do a fine job teaching us to use this area of our brains.

Spiritual Consciousness

Spiritual consciousness is the part of our mind and awareness that is different from the others. It operates, or we become consciously aware of it, only when the other parts are relatively still. Usually, it will not come into play when we are emotional or in great pain. It is a subtle function and operates under certain conditions.

Shifting Attention

One of the themes of this work has been that we have been taught to use our minds only in certain ways. An example of this is worrying. Most of us have had nights when we lie down to go to sleep and one worry after another pops into our head. It is like a TV set—on each station we flip to there is something else to worry about.

This repeating pattern can be stilled by the meditative exercises described earlier. We can shift attention and redirect it to another portion of our consciousness, which is calming and integrating.

This shifting of attention has been described in detail, with multiple examples. This technique has other values and uses; it is easily used as an antidote to worrying. Remember that this shifting of attention through meditation activity is only one form of spiritual exercise or technique. Throughout this book the traveler has been exposed to other states of consciousness (living in the moment, reflecting the light, prayer, and stilling everyday thought) and exercises to help foster this development. The great mystical poet Rumi said, "There are a thousand forms of mind." We in our culture are familiar with just a few. Many forms wait, undiscovered.

More Than This

I sometimes see abandoned cars on the Deegan. Someone leaves a car alongside the highway and scavengers pick it clean, taking off parts to sell or to use on their own car. All that remains is a carcass. Periodically, these wrecks are towed away to some junkyard, costing the taxpayer who knows how much.

This is the way of life. One day we are useful, and the next ready for the scavengers.

Yet we are more than this, and we must come to understand our òwn importance and usefulness. This is part of the learning that is necessary to make a complete person.

Strong Emotions

Last night some of us were sitting around the kitchen table, talking about how far we each had to drive to work. One of my daughter's friends remarked, "I hate that highway you drive to work . . . the Deegan. It's always backed up by the George Washington Bridge!"

I replied, "A lot of people feel the same way you do about it."

Later, I began thinking: it's not good to hate something too much; hating takes a lot of energy that can be expended in any number of more beneficial ways. It also blocks the higher consciousness.

Yet youth is full of strong emotions, and intense feelings have their place. The task is to become master of your emotions. Then you can use your emotions as tools instead of being controlled by them.

Music, Mood, and Easy Listening

In my professional training, I was exposed to early research about the effect of music on healing, mood, and shifting consciousness. Several of these initial studies measured the effects of different types of music pumped into hospital dayrooms as background sound. Often it was in these large, open spaces that patients rested, watched television, and spent many hours of their day.

Researchers quickly observed that listeners reacted physically and emotionally to different types of background music and sound. When classical music was played, the hospital patients often rested, and were tranquil and relaxed. In contrast, music with a heavy, repetitive, loud beat led some listeners to pace back and forth and even to strike out.

In the spiritual tradition that I am most familiar with, there are examples of teaching masters both cautioning disciples against listening to random forms of music and prescribing specific musical activity for spiritual development. For example, in order to evoke specific spiritual states, Rumi suggested that his disciples observe dancing activity (whirling dervishes), and Al-Hujwiri, in order to maintain spiritual balance, cautioned disciples against listening to music in indiscriminate and excitatory ways.

Both of these classical Masters were well versed in the effects that music has on mood and on spiritual learning. Under their direction, disciples were directed toward specific musical activity that would evoke and stimulate designated spiritual states.

Since commuters regularly listen to music, both discussions—about music's effect on mood and about its effect on spiritual learning—suggest the following points to consider:

- Music affects how we feel. It can calm and excite. It can be a factor in healing. On a daily commute, one must be sure to select music that will evoke the desired response. Fortunately, just about everyone recognizes the type of music they enjoy and that will be soothing and uplifting for them.

- People often unknowingly misuse spiritual pre-scriptions and attempt to randomly adopt tech-niques and activity prescribed for another time and place. Unfortunately, many times spiritual teachings do not translate well across time and cultures. According to one source, whirling der-vish dance and musical activity was originally prescribed for audience members, not the danc-ers. Additionally, it was prescribed for specific groups of disciples who needed to experience and expand specific emotional ranges.

- We all recognize musical pieces that are sooth-ing and spiritually uplifting. That is exactly the type of music required on an annoying commute. Commuters would be wise to plan ahead and have uplifting CDs and tapes readily available.

- If you require specific pieces of spiritually grounded music, I would direct you to your own spiritual tradition and suggest that you select pieces from that tradition that you or others like. If none are available, then you can select music you enjoy based upon the criteria and cautions I've listed above.

Imported Wisdom

I drive a Hyundai to work every day. It's a car made in Korea with a Japanese engine and transmission. I get about thirty-five miles per gallon on my five-speed.

Sometimes, things from the East are better than their Western counterparts. However, it is often a matter of taste that decides the issue.

The same is certainly true with religions and philosophical systems.

Creative Process

The Sufis claim that in order to free the higher consciousness, humanity must learn to use the mind in a different way. The creativity of the artist is the closest use of our brains to the higher consciousness.

In the creative process, the artist pulls together ideas and feelings in an inspirational moment of conscious energy. This intuitive grasp of things finds expression in an art form and depicts the artist's representation of reality.

This is one form of consciousness among many.

Misplaced Courtesy

If you ever drive on the Deegan during rush hour, the first thing that hits you is how discourteous the drivers can be. People usually cut each other off, and if someone sees you signaling to change lanes, often they speed up so you can't make the switch.

In this situation, it seems unnatural to be courteous. In fact, if you want to be courteous and repeatedly let others pull out in front of you, you'll never reach your destination on time.

Each situation has its own rules. The spiritual traveler must be flexible.

Student's Higher Potential

Driving south in the morning, I can sometimes smell the biscuits and cookies baking at the Stella D'Oro Company. They have a large plant alongside the Deegan. This fragrance evokes in me pleasurable visions of cakes and cookies waiting to be eaten.

Just as this fragrance calls forth a number of possibilities, so is the teacher able to perceive the student's fragrance, or potential for enlightenment.

Religions of Old

About two hundred yards south of the Washington Bridge, the High Bridge connects the Bronx and Manhattan. It was built solely for pedestrians and is constructed in part of fine beige bricks. Its design reminds me of a beautiful Roman aqueduct.

I've never seen anyone walking across this bridge. My mother told me when she was a girl people would take evening walks across it from Morris Heights, in the Bronx, to Highbridge Park.

Like the religions of old, this bridge's day has passed. However, its beauty still calls to all that is possible.

> *Knowing others is wisdom; knowing the self is enlightenment. Mastering others requires force; mastering the self needs strength. He who knows he has enough is rich. Perseverance is a sign of will power. He who stays where he is endures. To die but not to perish is to be eternally present.*
>
> —Lao Tsu

A Prophecy

There is a housing shortage in New York City, causing the rents for apartments to be astronomical. Yet as I drive on the Deegan, I see dozens of burned-out buildings. Some are being rehabilitated, and others wait for someone with a plan. Still, thousands remain homeless.

One day this will all come together. Each child will have a safe home, and everyone will wake up with the

Name of God on their lips. That is a prophecy in which humans will realize their true potential.

Strive for Personal Excellence

Duty to God and duty to humanity are similar. I drive the Deegan daily, so that I might go to work and join in the world's commerce, thereby supporting my family and contributing to everyone's welfare.

My capacity to fulfill worldly obligations is an indicator of how I will do in the spiritual realm.

If I am honest with myself and strive for excellence, it will be apparent in both worlds.

Being Prepared

Last week, as I was pulling onto the hospital grounds, my left rear tire suddenly went flat. I don't remember hitting a bump, and upon inspection it wasn't cut or punctured. The tire simply gave out. The rim cut the tire as I pulled into the parking lot with my flat.

Fortunately, I had a spare and the flat didn't occur on the Deegan. I was able to replace the tire with minimal effort.

In order to complete your journey, you must be prepared—and have a little luck.

Hearing the Call

Yonkers Raceway is the site of the Westchester County Fair. Driving south, I see the scores of amusement rides and booths that have been set up next to the racing area. The trotters are still able to practice; the fair is going on alongside the track.

For most of us, leisure is a time of choices and an opportunity to enjoy with others the things we like. It is a time for enriching our lives and for finding out who we are.

It was during a time of leisure that I first heard the call. At first, it was a very quiet yearning that eventually found a name. In all things there is the Divine.

Acceptance

This morning's 6:45 a.m. radio traffic report warned of late-running construction on the southbound Deegan just north of Fordham Road.

The traffic report advised drivers to take an alternate route. I didn't, as I was hoping the backup would be cleared by the time I reached the area. The construction was finished when I got there; however, the Deegan was backed up anyway. Rubberneckers checking out a police car and motorist north of Van Cortlandt Park and a backup at the ramps to the George Washington Bridge cost me another fifteen minutes of travel time.

Sometimes you just have to accept what is before you.

Croton Reservoir Bridge

Every morning I drive across a bridge that is part of the Taconic State Parkway. It is one of the most scenic spots that I have ever seen on any highway.

I occasionally see people who have hiked to the area to take photographs of the view across the Croton Reservoir, which is part of the reservoir system that feeds New York City its water supply. The reservoir is surrounded by lush green hills, and visitors can easily imagine they are in the middle of the Adirondack Mountains, gazing at a secluded lake.

In thirty minutes, as I continue my drive, I am gazing at thousands of buildings in the Bronx—what a contrast!

O Lord, is this diversity there to convince us You exist?

Hauling Food

All around me are anonymous truck drivers doing their jobs and hauling products throughout the metropolitan area. The average person receives no applause or fame for doing their job. The rewards are something other than that—a paycheck or a sense of contributing to the welfare of others. Most often we go about our days with little or no recognition; we are the quiet heroes.

In another realm, there is a similar group. These are the guardians of the Light, who work in total anonymity. They reflect the Light of the Universe, and without their guidance we would wither from spiritual starvation.

For Sale

After leaving the 7-Eleven, I drive down Underhill Avenue to the Taconic State Parkway. Underhill Avenue still has a lot of undeveloped land, and much of it is for sale.

A "For Sale" sign tells you a great deal about a culture. First, it implies that someone owns the land and by law can decide what to do with it. Also, the owner decides what the land is worth and whom to sell it to. These rights are passed on after death, in a will.

Yet in other cultures the concept of land ownership does not exist. American Indians lived on the land and were its caretakers. They considered the land a living organism that was part of the Earth Mother. How could anyone own a living thing?

Within each culture there are certain assumptions that become operating rules. In our culture we have glorified the needs of the individual, which has resulted in a materialistic or ownership frame of reference. The individual's needs are most important, and individuals can own or acquire many different things.

Neither of these cultural assumptions is good or bad. It is a matter of degree and balance. Both sets of assumptions call to different aspects of our consciousness. What is most important is that we understand this about ourselves, and are thereby able to utilize both sets of assumptions, finally learning to transcend them.

Knowing Right from Wrong

Driving down the highway, you quickly learn to watch out for police cars. They are cruising the road, looking to assist stranded motorists or serving as a warning to drivers to heed the traffic rules. They serve an important function; without their presence, it is likely the roads would be more chaotic.

Similarly, within each of us there are policing mechanisms. For the body, an example is pain. Within the ordinary consciousness, the voice of conscience suggests what is right or wrong.

When fully awakened on a spiritual level, intuitive perception is the certainty of one who knows. Sometimes this comes about via a quiet voice or an idea. Other times it comes in a flash of spiritual knowledge.

Spiritual Exercises and Experience

Keeping in mind the earlier discussions concerning the limitations of meditation, overdoing individual exercises, and self-prescribing, what types of spiritual experience can the average commuter realistically expect on a daily commute? *Remember—don't limit the possibilities!* Meditation is one technique, and these traveling tips are offered to help ensure a safe ride.

Spiritual experience is limitless and is its own yardstick, defying written, musical, or verbal description. As commuters are infinitely diverse, so too is their experience both individual and boundless. People know spiritual experiences because they have had them. Typically, like romantic love, spiritual experience is its own reward. It is personal, and it teaches us something and connects us with our Higher Self and the limitless creative potential of the Universe.

After you have gathered the items on your commuting lists, you should be practicing the exercises for no more than ten minutes per night over a limited time period. In this matter, it is not a question of the duration of the exercise but of its quality or effect. Once you have learned the skills, or if the exercise is not working for you, move on to other forms of learning. Remember to gradually add to your commute those exercises that you can do in a safe manner.

Follow your heart, religious teachings, and spiritual path. Into your commute integrate personal prayers, uplifting music, and songs to sing. When you are traveling to work and traffic backs up, you can turn to that part of self that is more tranquil, liberated, and a cosmic traveler. Remember: with a little practice and preparation, you can experience a few transcendent moments of spiritual peace as you travel to work. Potentially, these moments can be powerful enough to alter your commute and day.

- Feeling spiritual is not the same as being spiritual. Most people confuse emotional and psychological states with spiritual ones, remaining satisfied with fool's gold.

- Wisdom is not fine sayings or advice based upon previous experience. Wisdom is guidance and action that is in alignment with the Higher Plan.

MILE

7

Sufis, Service, and Prayer

The Path is none other than service of the people.

—Saadi

Throughout this book there are numerous references to the Sufis. Who are they? What do they claim or say?

The Sufis remain a mystery to most people. This is by design and function. First, Sufis do not call themselves Sufis. Others have given them this name. For someone who is studying "the Sufi Way," a more accurate description is *seeker*—someone who is seeking Truth.

For convenience in writing, I have been using the term *Sufi*, although it is inaccurate. Sufis are secretive. In order for them to do their work, they have disseminated information about themselves to the point that it confuses the average person. Some of this data appears to be contradictory. Also, because Sufis see their functions as multilayered and they have a variety of tasks to accomplish, they do not wish to be distracted by the curious or sensationally minded. Answering questions can become time-consuming and unproductive.

- According to Sufi tradition, humanity is evolving to a higher condition. This purposeful evolution is guided by a Plan and includes the awakening of certain capacities within each person. The guardians of this evolution and Plan have the responsibility to help direct and correct deviations.

- Humanity originated far beyond the stars and will one day return home. While in this realm, many possibilities exist. The highest or most noble is alignment with the Truth or Light.

- The Truth is the underlying unity of the Universe; it is the Mother and Father of us all. The Truth became manifest so it might be known and loved.

- With the awakening of certain capacities, additional abilities appear. Some term these *supranormal*. They are natural byproducts of another state of consciousness.

- To the Sufi, the most important thing on Earth is the protection and correct application of knowledge. This knowledge is acquired naturally through a guided course of study.

- In order for the seeker to be successful, there must be an alignment between the student, the teacher, and the Path. It is the grace of the Path that is the magical element.

- Teachers can instruct in any medium. In the past, they did so in a religious format. In America today, it is a scientific/psychological/self-help format. In other ages, poetry and alchemy were used.

- There has never been a time or community that has been without the teachers or enlightened ones. They are with us today and are our most precious resource.

- Because of the disharmony in the world today, a corrective must be added. This is the higher or spiritual knowledge. It is a nutrient that helps other capacities mature and expand.

- All paths are sacred and on an inner level united. It is only on an external level that they appear different.

- All aspects of consciousness are important. A balance must be struck between the many selves. The balancing factor is the higher consciousness.

- The course of study is multileveled and individual. The teacher sets the progression of exercises, readings, experiences, and other learning devices. It is always dependent on an assessment of the seeker's condition, and the teacher adds the corrective to create an independent, fully developed individual.

- The aim of the process is to develop integrated, completed human beings who participate in the world and have the capacity to see things from a spiritual perspective. This sight leads to correct action and what some have termed *human excellence*.

- This course of study is a science; it has been called *the Science of Man*. It was perfected thousands of years ago and involves elements of philosophy, psychology, art, science, and many other systems. Some claim that all these systems are outgrowths of the primordial, fundamental knowledge that the Sufi perceives.

To the uninitiated, these claims or statements may seem exaggerated, perhaps like something out of science fiction. Yet the Sufis would be the first to say, "Don't believe us. Test these statements yourself."

Attar of Nishapur stated, "The sea is still a sea, no matter the drop's philosophy."

Trained Extension of Consciousness

While driving to the Albuquerque airport, I remember my brother describing how traffic patterns mysteriously built up at a certain point on the highway. According to newspaper accounts, there was suddenly congestion with stop-and-go traffic for no observable reason. One moment the road was open, the next moment there was a traffic jam. Drive two miles or so on open road, and then traffic again. No accidents or stalled cars. To people there, this was a mystery.

My reply to my brother was simple. This was something I saw every day on the Deegan. When the number of cars on the road reaches a certain level around certain exits, there is a stop-and-go situation because of cars entering and leaving the highway. Just heavy traffic—nothing mysterious about it.

It is the same with higher studies. Abilities some claim are supranormal and mysterious are nothing more than a trained extension of consciousness.

Learning to Drive

When I was first learning to drive, my father did something really smart. Wanting to help me and realizing he wasn't the right one to teach me, he paid for driving lessons. Knowing we would argue, he wanted this situation to be positive and to work. So he hired a professional.

If you want to learn something, you have to go to the best person for the job.

It is the same with most things. Unfortunately, many people forget this fact and try to teach themselves. Such people are often the casualties of higher studies.

Sacrifice and Helping

One afternoon, when I came out of work at 4:30 p.m. and started up my car, the red warning light for oil came on. That morning, I had had my oil changed by one of those fifteen-minute places that specialize in oil changes.

After checking the oil level and inspecting the oil drainplug, I saw that I had no oil in my engine. Somehow I lost the plug on my ride to work.

What to do? Get my car towed? By whom? How would I get home?

Then I remembered Frank. He worked in the maintenance department and had helped me with my car one other time. He drove a Hyundai and was familiar with my model as well.

Fortunately, he was still at work, checking on various parts of his own car. What we had to do was go into the Bronx, find an auto-parts dealer who was still open after 5:00 p.m., and find the correct part. We went to four dealers before we found one open and bought a universal plug and enough oil to do the job. At this point, I breathed a sigh of relief.

When we got back to my car, it was about 6:00 p.m. So far, I had tied up about one-and-a-half hours of Frank's time, and his wife was waiting for him with dinner. When Frank started working on my car, one of the mechanics who worked at the hospital garage began to take an interest.

The hospital garage doesn't stock auto parts or oil, and it was closed for the night. He was on stand-by duty.

The universal plug didn't fit; we had bought the wrong one! What were we going to do now?

The hospital mechanic said, "Let me check inside." After about ten minutes, he came out with another plug—a little smaller, it didn't fit. This was going to be a long night. So much effort, all wasted.

Then Frank came up with an idea: wrap some latex around the fittings of the smaller plug. Frank went into the mechanical shop and began looking for some wrapping.

By this time, two hours had passed and my problem had involved at least three others: Frank, his wife, and the hospital mechanic. I was also sure my own family was beginning to worry a little.

Besides worrying about my car and how to get home, I was feeling bad for delaying Frank's dinner. He told me not to worry, and he good-naturedly kept searching for the solution to my problem.

Well, the latex wrapping around the smaller plug worked! I got home with just a little stress. Every twenty minutes or so, I pulled over to the side of the road to check if the oil drainplug was holding.

I paid Frank for his time and tipped the garage mechanic, but they really didn't have to help me. They did it because they wanted to do it. They helped me because I needed help, and they were happy to be of assistance.

There is something about helping others that makes us feel good. It draws us closer to Truth, and when sacrifice is involved something special happens.

"So I Can Help Others"

Before work one day, when I came out of the 7-Eleven with my coffee, I noticed an elderly disabled man sitting in a motorized golf cart-type vehicle. Clearly, he was panhandling, and I could see his legs were affected. The sign on his vehicle explained that he needed money to pay for his medication.

As I sat in my car sipping coffee, my inner voice told me to strike up a conversation with this fellow. So I got out of my car and asked him about his sign. Didn't his Medicare pay for the medication? He told me it pays for about 80 percent of it. His medication is $200 per month, and $40 is a lot of money for him.

Then he started telling me about the senior citizen center he goes to. Most of the people there don't have enough money for different things, so he asks for help so he can help others. The money he gets panhandling also goes to others. So I placed some money in his cup.

Driving away, two things struck me. Was it all a con job? I saw him holding a roll of singles after he took my dollars from the cup. Maybe he didn't really need all the money for his medication and to help others . . .

Yet the phrase "I ask for help so I can help others" may have had the ring of truth to it. Then again, maybe it was all part of the hustle . . . but I've spent my money in worse ways.

Helping Each Other

One day at work, one of my colleagues mentioned that our lives seem to be connected in some way. We have now worked with each other at two separate facilities over the past ten years. He wondered why.

I replied spontaneously, "So we can help each other."

He looked at me and sort of mumbled, "You may be right."

I walked away, knowing I was.

Anonymous Service

The Sufis assert that the highest form of service is self-less, anonymous service that is in alignment with the Truth.

Ordinary charity, or giving to others, is part of being a human being. Sufis believe it is something expected in everyday life, part of the basic social requirement of responsibility toward others. Furthermore, in order for the help to be most effective, it should be done in secret.

In our society, we most often make a display of generosity. Paintings that are donated to hospitals have a plaque with the donor's name on it. Lists of donors to a charity are published in newspapers.

This is a beginning and important; however, other higher levels of charity and giving exist. When the recipient knows the giver's identity, there is a risk of obligation. Giving that is free of obligation or a feeling of reward should be the goal. Giving must be out of the necessity of the situation.

Giving and Health

Research has begun to affirm the relationship between giving to others and good health. This is something that mothers of children could have told any of the scientists, saving them a great deal of time and energy. I remember my own mother saying that she never felt more alive than when she was raising her children. The role of a mother is to give and give.

We also hear the same thing from volunteers. They feel good when they are helping others. These good feelings are now thought to carry with them positive biochemical properties that reduce risk of infection, improve emotional health, and reduce stress.

When we are helping others, we focus on their problems and not our own. In the alchemy of the situation both parties benefit.

A Commuter's Reaction

A number of commuters have commented about the helpfulness of an earlier version of this *Guide* to their daily ride. For example, one New York City subway commuter described an experience she had one day on a particularly hot and crowded subway car.

She found herself pressed up against different travelers, barely able to keep her balance and grab the overhead handgrips. In one hand, she held her computer and business carryall, and with the other she strained to hold on to the overhead grip for dear life—while the train sped around one curve after another.

As she began to sweat, and as she bumped against different people, she cursed the ride, wanting it to end. Realizing she had another ten minutes to go under these conditions, she began to grow even more distressed. Then she remembered to control her thoughts and one of the concentration techniques offered here, and she began to intently focus on an overhead subway advertisement.

This colorful ad displayed two people frolicking on a distant sunny beach. Next, in her mind's eye, she pictured herself along with them, enjoying the sun and surf. Gradually, as she felt the sun and the ocean spray on her body, her attitude and her thoughts began to shift. And for a few moments, she was enjoying herself in a Caribbean paradise—no longer riding the crowded subway to work.

In spiritual wakefulness, it is not a matter of quantity of experience but of *quality*. A few glorious moments of clarity, such as those described above, can help change your commute, your day, and eventually your life.

Responsibility of Ownership

While possessions can be helpful in daily life, the more things you own, the more worries you have.

In our family we have four cars; the newest is a three-year-old Hyundai. It seems as if every week one of the cars needs some sort of maintenance, requiring time, energy, and money. This is a fact of responsibility and ownership.

———

Yet owning a car can also be joyous and fun. Think of the excitement you felt when you first brought home your new car. Or the enjoyable places you traveled in it with friends and family.

Owning a car increases the range of choices you have, and on one level provides a sense of freedom. You can work miles from your home and choose to live in any number of communities as a result—such is the mobility an automobile provides.

Car ads emphasize our need to feel free and do exciting things. They show cars on top of mountains, traveling through the jungle, or splashing through water by the ocean.

This plays to the desire we all have to break free of our worldly chains . . .

Real Freedom

Car ads are selling the illusion of freedom. For the moment you may feel free and on top of the mountain, but tomorrow the car payment is due or your daughter is sick and must be driven to the doctor.

Freedom, real freedom, is only found in your mind and consciousness. It is a state of awareness in which all the barriers and walls within your mind cease to bind. They have been removed by the Light of Truth, and anything is possible.

One day I was sitting in my friend's office, and we were discussing strategy on how to accomplish a volunteer activity. As I focused on the Light for guidance, I felt the walls within my mind disappear. The way I was thinking of solving the problem fit into a neat box with its limitations; that approach wasn't working.

Suddenly, as I focused on the Light, I felt the walls or barriers of my thought process fall down. Next came the solution to the problem. This approach worked.

———————

One day, the soul will leave the body. Then the soul will be free of earthly chains. While in the world of forms, we are to prepare for the next stage in the journey.

———————

The soul is housed in the body, and it often feels imprisoned by the thoughts we think and the chores of daily life. The remedy is to spend a few quiet moments every day focusing on the transcendent. Let your soul connect with its home far beyond the stars; your soul is imprisoned, wishing to continue with its journey.

————

In other cultures, it is expected that a traveler who reaches a certain level of capability will walk away from their daily routine and live by the beggar's bowl—going door to door, begging alms in the Name of the Beloved. Free from earthly responsibilities, such travelers can focus on another realm.

I remember when my teacher told me that if he were home in his own country, it would be expected he would do the same. In this culture, that was not the way. Here the way was different.

Rite of Passage

In our culture, driving a car is both a necessity and a rite of passage into adult life. If you have teenagers in your family, you know how much energy is expended around their desire to drive. They want to go places and do so many things, to experience the thrill of going and doing.

In time, the responsibility of ownership sets in. After a few car payments and a few minor fender-benders, some of the excitement is replaced with another aspect of reality.

Within Our Present Personality

In order to be useful, we must undergo a process of change. The Taconic Parkway is currently being widened. Trees and hills are being torn down so the highway can accommodate greater numbers of cars.

Among other changes, the engineers are taking large masses of stone from the hillsides next to the highway and pulverizing the stone into gravel. With a hundred yards of conveyor belts and machinery—and numerous dump trucks, cranes, and drills—they are changing tons of stone into gravel. This gravel becomes part of the foundation of the new road. One day the stone is a hill beside the road—the next day I am driving over it, going to work.

Such is the process with our present personality. Some of our thoughts and desires must be altered in order for the higher consciousness to operate.

Cathedral of Green

This spring has been particularly beautiful. The trees are deep green in color from all the rain and sunshine. As I drive down Underhill Avenue toward the Taconic, I notice the leaves on the trees have reached each other, about twenty feet above me. Branches from the opposite sides of the road have come together, forming a roof. Watching the sunlight filter through the limbs, I am reminded of a cathedral of green.

Surely, the architects of early churches must have gotten their designs from walking in the forests. Looking upward at the sunlight through a roof of green makes the soul want to sing.

Forms of Greed

Greed is an exaggerated concern for one's own need that usually results in harm to someone else.

We are all guilty of this at one time or another. Greed comes in hundreds of forms. Some people want money, others attention or power. Some of us crave spiritual attainment.

Because automobiles are essential to our way of life, hundreds of services have been created to meet this consumer need. Many of these services are overpriced; "buyer beware" is common knowledge when shopping for car-related services.

The price of new cars is so high that advertising specialists have created a term for it: *sticker shock*. By classifying this phenomenon (the consumer reaction to the high price of cars), it softens the blow. Then the consumer tempers his protest. After something is categorized, it is easier to understand.

There is an Oldsmobile dealership on Route 100, just before the entrance I use to get on the New York State Thruway. The lowest-priced new car advertised in their showroom window last month was equivalent to nearly two-thirds of the average American's yearly salary. How many people have that much money to buy a new car? Also, by the time you add tax and extras, you're looking at another 20 percent. Something is way out of line. Perhaps if prices were lower, people might buy more cars?

Yet not everyone who is in the automobile business is dishonest or looking to become rich at the consumer's expense. I have met honest mechanics and honest used-car salesmen.

Still, it does seem that something has gone wrong. Next to a home, cars are the second most expensive consumer item the average person buys.

When the price of auto parts is marked up 100 percent from wholesaler to retailer, and per-hour labor costs for car repairs are as much as the cost of seeing a doctor for an hour, you have to wonder how it will end.

Just as greed can consume a person, so can it consume an industry and nation. In all things a balance must be maintained.

A condition exists known as *spiritual greed*. It occurs when the traveler excessively seeks spiritual powers, states, or experiences. Spiritual greed sometimes results in the traveler neglecting worldly responsibilities or their own health. A sense of balance is destroyed by their desire to attain or accomplish.

Change Threshold

Last week there was another fuel spill on the southbound Deegan. It occurred by the 155th Street exit. All traffic reports urged drivers to take an alternate route.

I couldn't decide what to do. I was tired from working late the previous day, and I was in no mood to experiment with alternate routes. I wanted an easy, comfortable drive to work, but that wasn't going to be possible.

The situation demanded I react. So I took the Bruckner Expressway to the Triborough Bridge. It cost me an additional twenty minutes of travel time, but I had no choice. I had to alter my plans.

Then it occurred to me that this was the way most things got changed. People change only when they have to change. If we had a choice, most things would remain the same.

Self-less Service

The McLean Avenue exit is the last exit on the New York State Thruway, just before the highway turns into the Deegan. Sometimes as I drive by that exit I think about one of my old girlfriends. When I was in college I dated a young lady who lived near McLean Avenue. I visited her house in Yonkers a few times. Eventually we broke up; I wasn't ready for the commitment that was necessary.

In our culture, we have idealized romantic love. Songs, books, and television programs focus on idealized romantic love, glorifying its many aspects.

Yet to the spiritual traveler, romantic love is but the first step on the ladder. There are many forms of love, and most require a stronger commitment.

Romantic love is a beginning. Closer to the ultimate goal is the selfless devotion of a caregiver when someone is sick.

Exercise: A Perfect Prayer

Ultimately, prayer is communication between a person and that which is Highest. True prayer cannot be taught. Individual prayers can be. There should be no compulsion or fear in prayer. Prayer should be a spontaneous song—a joy, a celebration, and a stirring that arises from deep within your heart.

Many commuters often find themselves praying while traveling the roads, and asking for strength and guidance. As you travel, if it is your way, I would encourage you to pray and align your energy with that which is Highest and the Light, for it is the Light that dissipates commuting darkness.

In my own spiritual training, I was taught that within various spiritual traditions there are "perfect" prayers. That is, prayers that have everything in them necessary for the traveler to complete their journey. Within our tradition, the prayer of submission is one such vehicle. The following is my own personal version of this prayer, which I now share with you:

As the willow bends to the wind and the leaf curls to the rain, O Lord, I surrender myself to You.

Views on Prayer

Then a priestess said, "Speak to us of Prayer." And he answered, saying: "You pray in your distress and in your need; would that you might pray also in your fullness of your joy and in your days of abundance."

—Kahlil Gibran

Life Is the Prayer

For the Sufi, daily life and traveling down the highway is potentially a prayer. Every moment is an opportunity to align personal action with the Higher Impulse. Through intention and by temporarily surrendering individual need, the spiritual traveler makes their commute to work a prayer of joyfulness and service.

We were created to participate in everyday affairs, using our diverse range of skills to make the world better.

Let every action become a prayer. Let every moment bring you closer to your Higher Self and the Higher Destiny.

Prayer

Traveler: "Holy One, speak to me of prayer."

Master: "As the robin serenades the morning and offers thanks for another day, in this way prayer is a song that arises from the heart. As the mother caresses the baby and her heart swells with love, in this way prayer is sweeter than the rarest wine. As the sun travels the heavens and heralds the morning, in this way prayer is the work that we must do. Prayer takes endless forms, and many times we are confined to the ritual of praying. True prayer is performing all the tasks of the day as God's servant. Remember: we pray to the Beloved because *we* need God. The Most High does not need our prayers."

A Traditional Story

There is a very old story about a teaching Master who was traveling with a group of his students. They were in the process of making a spiritual journey, and their travels brought them to rest at an oasis. It was time for the midday prayer.

As the disciples prepared for their obligation and searched for a place to spread their prayer rugs, several of them noticed that just up ahead a baker was busy placing dough into an oven for bread. He seemed to be ignoring the hour; as he labored and sweated in the warm noon sun, he took several long, deep breaths to regain his strength, wiped his brow, and continued working.

This behavior puzzled and offended several of the students, causing one to speak to the Master concerning the baker's apparent disregard for the community obligation.

And this was the Master's reply, which has come down to us across the years: "This man's sighs are worth a thousand selfish prayers uttered out of vanity. Without rest this man labors to feed the weary traveler, and his actions constitute the higher service. He is one of the hidden friends, and his every breath is a joyful prayer and song to his Beloved."

— THOUGHTS FOR THE ROAD —

- When faced with stop-and-go traffic, it is easy to forget the open road. Yet both exist and follow one another.

- He or she is master who reigns supreme in their own Kingdom.

Higher Potential

You yourself are under your own veil.

—Hafiz

A Different View

Driving down the Deegan, just as you go under the overpasses for the George Washington Bridge, you can see the Empire State Building; it needs to be a clear day and you have to be in the left-hand lane and know where to look, but you can see it.

The columns of the pedestrian-only High Bridge serve as a decorative stone frame, setting off a magnificent view of the Manhattan skyline. Riding down the highway with steel overhead, you look in a certain direction and are filled with wonder . . . there it is, the Empire State Building.

I've told one of my friends at work about this view. He drives to work the same way I do and has been looking for weeks; he hasn't seen it yet.

Perhaps I am not describing it properly . . . or perhaps other factors are at work.

Being Grateful

When you feel sorry for yourself, practice gratitude and consider another who has been given less.

I know I have a difficult job. It is something I chose to do. Nevertheless, some days it makes me weary and I feel sorry for myself.

Every morning as I stop to pay the tolls by the Triborough Bridge, I see the newspaper sellers. They maneuver in and out of the stopped cars selling different newspapers. Rain or shine, they are out there hustling between the exhaust and stopped vehicles. In 20 degree weather or 100 degree weather, they are working.

Each person's life is filled with struggle and wonder. Perhaps to these newspaper sellers, this job is a beginning and an opportunity. To me it would be a greater burden.

Baggage Compartment

The other day I was reminded once again how similar people are to their cars. I met a fellow who began to tell me how he hated the way some people drove. He had just avoided an accident and was understandably distracted. Yet he started telling me about it in detail, without asking my name or if I was interested.

Just as cars have a trunk to carry luggage and groceries, so do we all carry around baggage—our memories, attitudes, and feelings concerning situations that are best left locked away or forgotten.

Knowing the Design

In reading over my list of some of the things that have happened while I drive to work, I am struck by the reoccurrence of certain situations. For example, I am often forced to change my route to work due to traffic conditions on the Deegan. My reactions are predictable . . .

So it is with many things in life. Situations have a structure or design to them. Our responses to these situations are often patterned the same, depending upon our personalities and conditioning.

The task is to be able to perceive the emerging structure or design of each specific situation, so we might become masters of the situation.

One of the Sufi Orders is called the Designers (*Naqshbandi*). Part of their training involves the use of stories as teaching instruments. In these stories, there is a structure or design that relates to psychological processes and events in everyday life. In learning these structures, students become able to relate these patterns to events taking place around them. Also, such learning sensitizes the student to look for patterns in behaviors and events. This is done so the student might transcend the situation.

Observing Others

You can learn a great deal about people just by watching and observing.

On my way to work today, a construction worker driving a Mack truck was racing down the highway. At first he was in the center lane; next he moved to the far-left passing lane. The last time I saw him, he was speeding in the right-hand lane, not allowing drivers to come onto the highway.

Next, a fellow on a motorcycle who was in a business suit was weaving in and out of stopped traffic. Everyone else was still, and he was using the space between vehicles to move ahead.

If you were to make some statements about these men and their personality traits, what would they be? Consider why each one selected the vehicle he was driving. Were you observing an isolated instance, or is this behavior typical of the way they drive and act every day?

There is an old story about one of the Servants of God who sold food from a street corner. One day a group of passing strangers stopped to buy some food from this man.

The vendor, through an inner awareness, immediately recognized his teacher by the way he ate his dinner. The prospective student gave up his stand and followed the Way as a result of this incident.

Years later, when questioned about that day, he said, "I had sold thousands of plates of food, but I had never seen anyone eat as my teacher did."

Obviously the teacher displayed a grace and bearing that called to the student, even in this minor act.

Watch people and watch your reaction to them. You will learn a great deal from both. This can be done as your car is stalled in traffic.

Knowing Self

Each of the high-rise apartment buildings that border the Deegan is a small world. Some of them house hundreds of families. People living on the thirtieth floor often don't know their neighbors who live on the second floor.

Within each personality there are hidden places— what person can claim that they know every aspect of themselves?

Yet in the journey, the higher consciousness will operate within the ordinary personality. Often it is a matter of removing something rather than of adding something.

Certain thoughts and patterns block other things from happening, just as certain traffic events and patterns block the progress of others.

Necessity

Having to do something is much different than wanting to do something. I have to drive to work every day, but it is not something I want or choose to do.

That which we have to do is essential, like eating, loving another, and working; these needs spring from our basic human nature. Those things we want to do may or may not be essential—for example, going on vacation to a sunny climate or becoming a millionaire. We may want a vacation and the money to pay for it. The range of choices about location and how much to spend are variable.

Those who attain, or reach the goal of spiritual completion, are those who *have* to travel. For them there is no other choice.

In our lives, there are many things over which we have control and choice. Similarly, there are others for which no choice is available.

In both situations, the individual's will is involved: that which is tied to the transcendent is primary and by necessity a reality (e.g., death); that which is tied to desire or want may or may not be necessary.

On the Path, the traveler learns to put aside those things that are both essential and optional to experience the next level of consciousness.

What difference does it make if I want to go to work or I have to go to work? I am driving the Deegan, yet I seek to experience something higher.

———

The magical part of our personality or consciousness is our will. When we have to do something—that condition where want has been extended to absolute necessity—an extra level of energy is created.

This energy seeks a conduit, and things begin to happen.

Embrace the Moment

All we have is this moment—no one is promised another day. Make the best of it.

No matter if you are driving your car, reading this book, or doing any number of other activities, all you have is the present. Yesterday is a memory, and tomorrow is a promise that may or may not come true.

The task is to use what you have and enjoy this opportunity. You are a flower waiting to bud. You are a potential about to mature. Use this moment to grow closer to your dreams.

Within each person, there is a capacity that seeks ultimate truth or reality. During a person's life, this capacity will attach itself to many things, and many roads will be taken. Finally, one day the proper conduit is found and the journey begins in earnest. Like calls to like, and the spiritual journey begins.

Maximize Your Potential

Make your life the prayer. Seek to make each moment a declaration of love and goodness. Be kind to yourself so you can be kind to others. Be honest with yourself so you can be honest with others. Maximize your own potential so you can help others to maximize theirs.

————

In this age, the Ancient Wisdom wears the garment of exploration of self and the expanded use of our minds.

It is the same journey, but today's circumstance dictates we drive at sixty miles per hour.

Balancing Factor

Sometimes it is really clear that we are killing ourselves.

This week, record temperatures are being set in New York City and the nearby region. Temperatures have been in the high 90s and low 100s Fahrenheit. In addition to the heat, it has been nearly impossible to breathe because of the humidity and pollution.

Driving down the Deegan, I can see the pollution in the air. Next to the Stella D'Oro factory there is a large sign with the current temperature: 79°—at 7:15 a.m.

Since the air quality is so poor, people are being advised to stay indoors. Our air conditioner at home has been running nonstop for a week. Even with energy efficiency ratings, all these air conditioners have to be contributing to the pollution and heat. Certainly this is true with automobiles; when you run your car's air conditioner, your engine runs hotter and with more emissions.

This is a vicious cycle. It's hot outside so we run a machine to cool things down; in doing so, we create more heat and pollution. How will the cycle be broken?

———

What is the corrective to these problems? What can the average person do?

Historically, all civilizations have had a period of decay. Furthermore, nature has shown us, through the extinction of various species, that we must adapt or die. We are quickly reaching this point.

The missing ingredient, however, is the higher consciousness and its integrating effects. This is the antidote to excess; it helps balance concern for self with concern for others. The higher consciousness pulls together all the parts and helps to redirect energy toward the greater good.

What the world needs are better people: people who do their jobs well and who are as concerned about others as they are about themselves, people who know the meaning of moderation and the dangers of excess, people who know which things they have control over and which things must be left to others.

You might ask how the "golden rule" applies to today's world and the problems of pollution and depletion of the ozone layer.

The balance has been destroyed by greed and excess. The corrective is to bring each life into balance—then each person's energy can be directed for the greater good. Good citizens lead to a good world. People all doing their jobs well and helping others . . . the balance will be restored!

Deegan as Metaphor

To me, driving the Deegan is a metaphor. The Deegan represents that which is both good and bad about our society. The road is old and falling apart, yet it provides opportunity for millions.

We have forgotten the missing ingredient and given away the control we do have. Governments cannot solve our problems; people solve problems. Good people make good governments.

So when the traffic is backed up, the horns are blaring, and your children are asking, "When are we getting there?" turn inward. Use the techniques presented in this book, and in time the higher consciousness will awaken.

This capacity cannot get you out of the traffic, but it can make your ride a different one. You will also begin to understand how this capacity integrates other functions. Then, as you are in balance, the world will begin to be a little better.

Deep Breathing and Relaxation

Over the past twenty-five years, much has been written about the relationship between deep breathing, which gets more oxygen to the brain, and the control of specific bodily functions that counter rising anxiety levels. In fact, this information and awareness has percolated through our society to the point where it is now common knowledge.

From a spiritual perspective, breath is life. The basic breathing motion—taking in a slow deep breath, holding the breath for a short count, and exhaling slowly out—represents the primal motion of the soul going out into the Universe, staying in this world, and returning home. This in-and-out movement—breathing in, holding it for a time, and exhaling out—parallels the soul's entrance in the physical world, living our lives, and traveling out at the point of death. Additionally, this in-and-out motion is believed by many to align with basic sexual movement, which helps create life itself.

Well, enough of esoteric explanations. Let's turn our discussion back to the daily commute. If I find myself growing anxious, which often happens while I'm driving my car, and my heart begins to beat faster and adrenalin starts flowing due to an anticipated annoying situation or emerging traffic slowdown, I take two deep breaths to help me relax, calm down, and return to a point of balance. This breathing activity also helps me to interrupt and break my train of thought, which is what gave rise to my growing anxiety levels.

Many people have a favorite deep-breathing exercise, and it is not the point of this discussion to get you to replace what has been useful for you. Instead, I simply want to point out that deep breathing can help balance you and reduce your stress during your daily commute. I also want to share that over the years I have consciously added another level to my deep-breathing activity.

As I inhale and exhale while breathing deeply, I repeat one of the Names of God or a focus word (*Yah /weh, Al/lah,* or *sun/shine*). This consciousness-raising activity helps add a spiritual dimension or Light to the breathing exercise. When I breathe in through my nose, I slowly repeat in my mind the first half of the name/

word (*Yah*, *Al*, or *sun*), and when I exhale slowly, out through my mouth, I repeat on my breath the second half of the name/word (*weh*, *lah*, or *shine*).

For travelers who have never used a breathing exercise, I suggest, for practical and safety reasons, growing familiar with the following exercise at home before trying it on your ride in to work.

Holy Name Breathing Exercise

Sit with good posture in the seat of your car, or on a bus, train, or plane. Breathe in slowly through your nose and simultaneously repeat in your mind the first part of your focus word (*Yah*, *Al*, or *sun*).

Inhale deeply, filling first the lower part and then the upper part of your lungs. Try to time the first half of your word with your breath. Hold your breath for three to four seconds. Exhale slowly out through your mouth, repeating on your breath the second half of the focus word (*weh*, *lah*, or *shine*).

Next, relax your abdomen and chest. Wait five seconds and repeat this exercise one more time. Do not overdo it, or you will become lightheaded.

If you already use a deep-breathing exercise, I suggest that you add a focus word. In time, with a little practice, this combination of factors will add another level to what you are doing.

— THOUGHTS FOR THE ROAD —

- The book of your life is filled with many blank pages. You are free to write on them whatever you choose.

- Man is the creator of many of his own problems, giving too much credit to God in this regard— while unaware of those areas in which God actually works.

MILE

8.5

Parting Thoughts

Wheresoever ye turn, there is the face of God.

—The Koran

Flexibility and Stretching

Looking back across my years of commuting, here are the top five things I have learned:

- As universally understood, the number one lesson: don't commute unless you must.

- If your job is a distance away and there is a choice of transport, pick the ride that is most enjoyable, efficient, and that best suits your temperament.

- Learn flexibility. Incorporate different activities, strategies, traveling partners, and spiritual practices to make the situation work.

- In life, many activities can teach you to stretch yourself and learn different things. Commuting is one of these activities.

- Finally, in everything there is the Divine. Yes, even in your irritating commute to work. Remember the ancient words of wisdom from the Koran: "Wheresoever ye turn, there is the Face of God."

Parting Thoughts

Well, it's almost time for me to drop you off. We are approaching your stop. A few parting thoughts before I continue on:

To me, the Deegan is like my life and mind. Some days, the ride is straightforward with no problems. Other days, there is a fuel spill, an accident, or drivers are cutting in and out. Some days, order; some days, chaos.

The thoughts, anecdotes, and solutions presented in this book were, at times, not in any particular order. Themes were scattered about like a stream of consciousness. There was a beginning and end. The pages in the middle were filled with different things. Some of which I chose. Some of which chose me.

I hope you enjoyed the ride and that you will take from it what is useful for you. Because that was the point, to provide something of use.

Until we meet again.

- Yesterday you were a caterpillar. Today you are a butterfly. Tomorrow what will you become?

A Lock of Hair

Traveler: "Master, please explain to me how the average person may know of what we experience. When I consider speaking with the members of my family and trying to relate to them some of our spiritual teaching, I fear my explanation will fall short and not convince them to follow our Way."

Master: "The question you raise is a multilevel one and presumes we have a duty to convince others to follow our Way; that is not so. God or the Light is all-loving and has created a way for each person to draw closer. The Path we follow is our Way, because we are called to follow it. Does God love one child more than another?

"In time, all travelers have an individual experience of God—some in this world, and others in the next. This matter is beyond our control or understanding. Yet in this matter, it is love that rules. Do not fear: all will receive full measure.

"In our journey along the Path, travelers who have a spiritual experience are instructed to keep it to themselves or inform only their teacher. To share it with others may create envy and even distrust. Also, spiritual experience is given so that the traveler may learn something and draw closer, not so the traveler may feel important or believe they have gained something special.

"Finally, all of these experiences, no matter how exciting, are not the goal. They are fore-tastes, miniscule passing aspects of the greater spiritual reality. These states and experiences are not the Light, and they may be compared to a lock of hair that has fallen off a beautiful maiden. No matter how fine, shiny, and colorful, these few strands of hair are but a minor aspect of the maiden's entire beauty and reality."

Traveler: "If what you say is true, then what is the benefit of spiritual experience or reading and studying any of the great books that help point the way? Being only small representations of what is possible, what purpose do they serve?"

Master: "This world was created so everything in it might sing glory to the Light. It is the nature of the Light to give and give. In this matter, we cannot limit the potential of events, discussions, books, and spiritual experience. For the tired traveler, each is a potential caress and helps point the way home.

"If someone questions you about your Path, be open and share with them; however, do not debate or try to convince them. We are not looking for converts. Our Way is other than this."

REFERENCES

Introduction *Getting Ready for the Ride*

p. xiii: The quote is from "Some Wise Sayings of Holy Prophet Mohammad," http://www.geocities.com/ahlulbayt14/SayingsProphet.html (accessed 29 August 2007).

p. xviii: Caren Halbfinger, "Author Finds Enlightenment in Traffic on Major Deegan," *The Journal News* (White Plains, NY), 27 October 2004.

p. xxii: Information about the Major Deegan Expressway from "Major Deegan Expressway: Historic Overview," www.nycroads.com/roads/majordeegan/ (accessed 10 March 2007).

Mile 1   *The Ride Begins*

p. 1: The quote appears in "The Sufi Quest" by Mev-levi Ustad Hilmi, quoted in Idries Shah, *Thinkers of the East* (New York: Penguin, 1987), and is cited in Robert Cecil, Richard Rieu, and David Wade, *The King's Son*. London: Octagon Press, 1981, 9.

pp. 11–12: Census information from "U. S. Census Bureau News: American Community Survey Releases," http://www.census.gov/acs/www/ (accessed 10 March 2007).

Mile 2   *Signs, Learning, and Life*

p. 25: Idries Shah, "Sufi Spiritual Ritual and Beliefs," from Idries Shah, *Sufi Thought and Action*. London: Octagon Press, 1990, 1.

pp. 37–38: Information about commuting from "Commuting," Wikipedia, www.en.wikipedia.org/wiki/Commuting (accessed 10 March 2007).

p. 39: William Blake, *The Portable Blake*. Edited by Alfred Kazin. New York: Viking, 1968, 150.

Mile 3 *Happiness and Everyday Experience*

p. 49: The Rumi quote appears in Shah, *Sufi Thought and Action*, 44.

p. 62: The Lao Tsu quote appears in Lao Tsu, *Tao Te Ching*, translation by Gia-Fu Feng and Jane English. New York: Random House, 1972, chapter 58.

Mile 4 *Opening the Door*

p. 71: This quote appears online at "Dhamma-pada—Sayings of Buddha (translated by J. Rich-ards)," http://www.edepot.com/dhamma2.html (accessed 29 August 2007).

pp. 92–93: "Major Deegan Expressway: Historic Overview" (accessed 10 March 2007).

Mile 5 *Way of the Heart*

p. 103: This quote appears online at "Muhammad Baha'uddin Shah Naqshband May Allah Bless His Secret and Sanctify His Soul," http://www.naqshbandi.org/chain/17.htm (accessed 29 August 2007).

pp. 105–107: Herbert Benson and Miriam Z. Klipper, *The Relaxation Response*. New York: Avon, 1976.

pp. 105–107: Herbert Benson and William Proctor, *Beyond the Relaxation Response*. New York: Berkley Books, 1985.

p. 107: The quote from Al-Hujwiri appears in Idries Shah, *The Way of the Sufi* (New York: Penguin, 1991) and Cecil, Rieu, and Wade, *The King's Son*, 137.

p. 113: Robert E. Ornstein, *Multimind*. Boston: Houghton Mifflin, 1986.

Mile 6 *States of Mind*

p. 125: The Rumi quote appears in Idries Shah, *The Sufis*. London: Octagon Press, 1989.

p. 132: Al-Hujwiri, *Kashf al-Mahjub: "The Revelation of the Veiled,"* An Early Persian Treatise on Sufism, translated by Reynold A. Nicholson. Oakville, CT: David Brown Book Co., 2000.

p. 137: Lao Tsu, *Tao Te Ching*, chapter 33.

Mile 7 *Sufis, Service, and Prayer*

p. 147: The Saadi quote appears in Idries Shah, *Knowing How to Know*. London: Octagon Press, 1998, 217.

p. 173: The Gibran quote appears in Kahlil Gibran, *The Prophet*. New York: Knopf, 1968, 67.

Mile 8 *Higher Potential*

p. 179: The Hafiz quote appears in Idries Shah, *Knowing How to Know*, 220.

Mile 8.5 *Parting Thoughts*

p. 197: This quote from the Koran (2:115) appears online at "Wahiduddin's Web, The Eyes of the Heart," http://wahiduddin.net/views/eyes_of_the_heart.htm (accessed 4 December 2007).

Free Catalog

Get the latest information on our
body, mind, and spirit products!
To receive a **free** copy of Llewellyn's consumer
catalog, *New Worlds of Mind & Spirit*, simply call
1-877-NEW-WRLD or visit our website at
www.llewellyn.com and click on *New Worlds*.

LLEWELLYN ORDERING INFORMATION

Order Online:
Visit our website at www.llewellyn.com, select your books, and order
them on our secure server.

Order by Phone:
- Call toll-free within the U.S. at 1-877-NEW-WRLD
  (1-877-639-9753). Call toll-free within Canada at
  1-866-NEW-WRLD (1-866-639-9753)
- We accept VISA, MasterCard, and American Express

Order by Mail:
Send the full price of your order (MN residents add 6.5% sales tax) in
U.S. funds, plus postage & handling to:

Llewellyn Worldwide
2143 Wooddale Drive
Woodbury, MN 55125-2989

Postage & Handling:
Standard (U.S., Mexico, & Canada). If your order is:
$24.99 and under, add $3.00
$25.00 and over, FREE STANDARD SHIPPING

AK, HI, PR: $15.00 for one book plus $1.00 for
each additional book.

International Orders (airmail only):
$16.00 for one book plus $3.00 for each additional book

Orders are processed within 2 business days.
Please allow for normal shipping time. Postage and handling rates subject to change.

Discover Your Spiritual Life

Illuminate Your Soul's Path

ELIZABETH OWENS

Many people are led to the spiritual path by a mystical experience, by a tragic life circumstance, or by nagging feelings of discontent. Whatever the reason, you need a road map or guide to assist you along the way. Spiritualist medium Elizabeth Owens gives you the tools to connect with that higher guidance that, she says, already resides within yourself.

Learn a life-changing method for handling problems and disappointments. Discover effective ways to meditate, pray, create affirmations, forgive those who have hurt you, and practice gratitude. Process painful emotions and thoughts quickly through the art of becoming a balanced observer.

ISBN: 978-0-7387-0423-4

216 pages

$12.95

The Fresh Start Promise
28 Days to Total Mind, Body, Spirit Transformation

EDWIGE GILBERT

Everyone has the impulse for a new beginning—a fresh start. Whether your motivation is weight loss, stress reduction, recovery, or simply a lasting feeling of joie de vivre, this 28-day program can help you change your life . . . permanently.

Transform your mind, body, and spirit in just four weeks! With unique French flair, Edwige Gilbert offers a lasting program for personal change and spiritual growth that requires just twenty minutes twice a day. Dispel fears and negative thoughts that obstruct your vision of change. Tap into the universal healing energy known as Qi (chi) for vitality and enthusiasm to pursue your goal. Discover your talents and gifts and reconnect with your true self.

Gilbert's inspiring makeover concludes with a plan to strengthen your new conditioning, achieve future goals, and maintain a life of laughter, love, and peace.

ISBN: 978-0-7387-1322-9
288 pages

$17.95

To order, call 1-877-NEW-WRLD
Prices subject to change without notice

Get Out of Your Way
Unlocking the Power of Your Mind
to Get What You Want

LAYTON PARK

Beliefs, dreams, fears, goals—they all begin in the mind. Hypnosis offers a way to tap into the subconscious mind to produce amazing life changes.

From professional sports to the business world, hypnosis has helped millions achieve their desires. In *Get Out of Your Way*, Layton Park explains how and why hypnosis works and shares "universal laws of mind" for transforming our belief system to allow our dreams to come true. Readers will learn how to clarify goals, construct effective affirmations, and engage these affirmations for positive life-changing results. Also featured are compelling case histories—true stories from the author—demonstrating the success of self-hypnosis.

Included with the book is an audio CD of easy-to-follow self-hypnosis techniques that can be used for accomplishing career goals, losing weight, quitting smoking, resolving phobias, and fulfilling a wide variety of personal ambitions.

ISBN: 978-0-7387-1052-5

216 pages

$21.95

To order, call 1-877-NEW-WRLD
Prices subject to change without notice

Real Steps to Enlightenment
Dynamic Tools to Create Change

AMY ELIZABETH GARCIA

Connecting with the divine is crucial for spiritual advancement, but choosing a spiritual path is anything but easy.

Amy Elizabeth Garcia simplifies the journey to enlightenment into thirty-three spiritual goals, such as finding your life purpose, developing trust in the universe, relinquishing the need to control, recognizing synchronicity, and fostering peace. Focusing on a specific spiritual lesson, each chapter begins with a divine message from the author's spiritual master that includes stories from his human incarnations. Garcia goes a step further in bringing these concepts to life by sharing her own life experiences. Every chapter includes a prayer inspired by angels and exercises for spiritual growth—the perfect complement to this beginner's guide to enlightenment.

Amy Elizabeth Garcia is a Reiki Master who receives guidance from her angels, healing guides, and the Master Jesus as she channels the Christ Force energy. She teaches workshops and conducts intuitive counseling and energetic healing sessions.

ISBN: 978-0-7387-0896-6

264 pages

$14.95

To order, call 1-877-NEW-WRLD

Prices subject to change without notice

Sacred Signs
Hear, See & Believe Messages
from the Universe

ADRIAN CALABRESE, PhD

When author Adrian Calabrese's father was in surgery for a life-threatening medical condition, she asked for a sign that he would survive—and she received one. Now she shares her secrets for getting clear guidance from the Universe in *Sacred Signs*, teaching a simple three-step method for receiving divine messages.

Unlike other books on the subject, *Sacred Signs* is not a "sign dictionary." Calabrese believes that the interpretation of a sign is as unique as the individual receiving it. The original checklists and questionnaires throughout the book help readers focus their desires, and success stories provide inspiration and further demonstrate how to use this personal, nondenominational approach to interpreting divine signs.

Adrian Calabrese, PhD, holds a doctorate in Psychical Research, another in Metaphysics, and is a certified clinical hypnotherapist. She is an intuitive counselor, minister, and inspirational speaker.

ISBN: 978-0-7387-0776-1

216 pages

$13.95

To order, call 1-877-NEW-WRLD
Prices subject to change without notice

Sail into Your Dreams

8 Steps to Living a More Purposeful Life

KAREN MEHRINGER

Sail into Your Dreams is the perfect book for anyone who's ever asked, "Is this all there is to life?"

Unsatisfied with her busy life in Seattle, Karen Mehringer embarked on a six-month, life-changing ocean odyssey to Australia, Indonesia, Fiji, and, most importantly, toward the joyful, fulfilling life she had always wanted.

You don't have to leave land to make your dreams come true. Karen shares the wisdom and practical tools she learned on her ocean odyssey, showing us how to focus on what truly matters. Journal entries and inspiring stories from Karen and others highlight how to slow down, nurture yourself, connect with others, and tap into your life force energy—the source of infinite possibilities.

This eight-step program will help you assess your life and eliminate toxic relationships, emotional trauma, physical clutter, and debt—making space for new experiences that awaken your passion and spirit.

ISBN: 978-0-7387-1053-2

240 pages

$13.95

To order, call 1-877-NEW-WRLD

Prices subject to change without notice